B6
14.50

P9-AQP-759

JZ 1479 .L45 1976

Leigh, Michael, 1949-

Mobilizing consent : public opinion and
American foreign policy, 1937-1947.

18879

DATE DUE

Mobilizing Consent

MOBILIZING CONSENT

Public Opinion and American Foreign Policy, 1937-1947

MICHAEL LEIGH

GREENWOOD PRESS
Westport, Connecticut • London, England

Library of Congress Cataloging in Publication Data

Leigh, Michael. 1948-
    Mobilizing consent.

    Bibliography: p.
    Includes index.
        1. United States—Foreign relations—1933-1945—Public opinion. 2. United States—
Foreign relations—1945-1953—Public opinion. I. Title.
JX1417.L39   301.15'43'32773   75-44656
ISBN:0-8371-8772-9

Copyright © 1976 by Michael Leigh

All rights reserved. No portion of this book may be reproduced, by any process or technique, without the express written consent of the publisher.

Library of Congress Catalog Card Number: 75-44656
ISBN:0-8371-8772-9

First published in 1976

Greenwood Press, a division of Williamhouse-Regency Inc.
51 Riverside Avenue, Westport, Connecticut 06880

Printed in the United States of America

FOR SCARLET

Contents

Preface

This book is the product of two research interests: the clash between the so-called traditional and radical interpretations of American foreign policy and the impact of public opinion on national decision making. These two interests merge in the debate concerning the role of public opinion in the major reorientations of American foreign policy that culminated in the cold war. The traditionalist argues that American policy makers are constrained by public opinion. The radical replies that mass apathy and indifference enable policy makers to manipulate public opinion in favor of their predetermined policy choices. Such manipulation is less coercive than downright repression of the authoritarian kind, but the effect is more or less the same.

This book challenges these rival interpretations. It attempts to disentangle the manipulation-versus-constraint controversy by piecing together the linkages between mass opinion and decision making. This difficult task is undertaken in the concrete setting of major shifts in policy that have been hailed as classic cases of "manipulation" or of the public-opinion "constraint." Although rooted in specific case studies, the book's conclusions rest on an analytic framework that is capable of wider generalization. Chapter 1 provides a set of rules indicating the probability of the participation of mass opinion in decision making. These rules are as applicable to contemporary foreign policy as to the cases under detailed scrutiny in this book.

The advantages of selecting decisions made several decades ago as test cases for the impact of public opinion lie principally in the availability of sources. This study draws on documents whose contemporary equivalents, if they exist at all, are stowed well out of sight of the curious researcher. Particularly useful are the unpublished in-house reports on the activities of wartime agencies in the public-opinion business, such as

OWI, which have not surfaced elsewhere in the literature. Equally interesting, both for the data they contain and for their insights into presidential thinking about public opinion, are the unpublished notebooks of Hadley Cantril. Chapters 3 and 4 include an analysis of the role of this pioneer in persuading the White House and the Department of State of the relevance of poll data to foreign-policy decisions.

If we are to take up the challenge and elucidate the linkages between public opinion and foreign policy there is no alternative to a research strategy that uses the traditional tools of both political scientist and historian, for without documentary research we can say little about the inner workings of government, and without public-opinion data the popular mood remains a subject for conjecture.

In preparing this study I had the advantage of critical comment from Lincoln Bloomfield, Ithiel de Sola Pool, and Donald Blackmer of the Department of Political Science, Massachusetts Institute of Technology. They read the entire manuscript in its early drafts and made many invaluable suggestions concerning form and content. Other friends and colleagues at MIT, Wellesley College, and the University of Sussex contributed indirectly to the progress of the manuscript through frequent discussions of related topics. Esther Leigh provided some useful editorial suggestions, which are reflected in the final manuscript. My wife Scarlet valiantly prepared the bibliography, battling with what was then for her a new language. Jackie Sobel typed the first complete draft of the manuscript and gave generous assistance in preparing it for dispatch to the publishers. Sylvia Burton typed part of the final draft with great speed and accuracy.

Thanks are also due to the staffs of the Franklin Delano Roosevelt Library, the Harry S. Truman Library, the University of Virginia Library, the Library of Congress and the Roper Public Opinion Research Center for facilitating my access to their archives.

I wish to thank the trustees of the John F. Kennedy Memorial Trust for providing a scholarship that made it possible for me to begin my research at the Massachusetts Institute of Technology.

For any errors of fact or judgment, I am, of course, responsible.

Abbreviations

AID	Agency for International Development
AIPO	American Institute of Public Opinion
CIAA	Co-ordinator of Inter-American Affairs
CIA	Central Intelligence Agency
CPI	Committee on Public Information
CR	*Congressional Record*
DOI	Division of Information
DPI	Division of Press Intelligence
FIS	Foreign Information Service
IMF	International Monetary Fund
NORC	National Opinion Research Center
NRA	National Recovery Administration
OCD	Office of Civilian Defense
OEM	Office of Emergency Management
OFF	Office of Facts and Figures
OGR	Office of Government Reports
OPA	Office of Public Affairs
OPOR	Office of Public Opinion Research
OWI	Office of War Information
SWNCC	State-War-Navy Co-ordinating Committee
USIS	United States Information Service

Introduction

MANIPULATION VERSUS CONSTRAINT: AN INTRODUCTION

Diplomatic history has shed considerable light on the degeneration of the Grand Alliance of World War II and its replacement by a hostile, polarized relationship between the United States and the Soviet Union. But in its long preoccupation with the subject, it has been sidetracked into an academic debate that involves nearly as much vituperation and distortion as the cold war itself.[1]

Some historians have reacted against the sterility of this debate by approaching the problem from a different angle, one that stresses the perceptual elements in decision making and that operates primarily at the national level of analysis.[2] This approach recognizes that the formulation of foreign policy occurs within a domestic context whose political imperatives often appear more salient than those of the international situation to the policy maker. It does not impute greater potency to domestic than to world dynamics in generating the cold war. Rather it suggests that some of the necessary conditions of that conflict, hitherto largely neglected, can be discovered in the domestic context.

Once the national level has been selected, it is a short step to the perceptions of policy makers; for, as J. David Singer observes, "If the nation is seen as a group of individuals operating within an institutional framework, then it makes perfect sense to focus on the phenomenal field of those individuals who participate in the policy making process."[3]

Of all the perceptions that impinge on the decision maker, democratic theory, as well as the comments of statesmen and scholars, attributes a special importance to public opinion. "In a democracy the People are entitled to determine the Ends or general aims of foreign policy," said Lord Bryce.[4] Many American scholars maintain that this normative principle is implemented in the formulation of United States foreign policy. "What the government in Washington does or fails to do in the field of foreign affairs will depend largely on the wishes of our citizens," Thomas Bailey wrote in the early days of the cold war.[5] Even scholars who doubt the normative principle Bryce advanced have confirmed Bailey's empirical observation. Walter Lippmann preferred to trust diplomacy rather than the popular mood in judging the wisdom, the necessity, or the expediency of a policy departure. But he did not doubt that "at critical junctures, when the stakes are high, the prevailing mass opinion will impose what amounts to a veto upon changing the course upon which the government is at the time proceeding."[6]

If, as a matter of principle or simply of practice, mass opinion does determine the ends or the outer limits of the nation's foreign policy, the traditional scholar insists that that opinion be enlightened. Government carries the obligation of informing and educating the public about the conduct of American diplomacy. Such education is entirely legitimate and does not amount to manipulation. The president "has a responsibility to lead public opinion as well as respect it—to shape it, to inform it, to woo it, and win it."[7]

Here the radical critic scents empty democratic ritual at best and hypocrisy at worst. He argues that the public has little discernible influence on the decisions of the foreign-policy bureaucracy. Public opinion is characterized by its apathy and indifference to external events. In this pliable state it scarcely acts as a *constraint* on policy makers. On the contrary, it is *manipulated* to conform with predetermined policy choices, which reflect the class interests of the foreign-policy elite. Opinion management differs only in technique in democratic and authoritarian political systems: "In a society without serious opposition, manipulation replaces the knout."[8] Popular languor makes manipulation rather than downright coercion the normal "democratic" form of opinion management.

With the exhaustion of economic determinism as a subject of fruitful debate, these rival interpretations of the impact of public opinion have assumed greater prominence in contending analyses of American foreign policy. But neither side has troubled to specify the linkages between what the public believes and how policy makers behave. They fail to explain systematically how public opinion is crystallized, transmitted to, and interpreted by the people at the top of the foreign-policy bureaucracy. The student who pursues claim and counterclaim in search of empirical verification usually finds only metaphor. Policies must be "tried before the court of public opinion" or "sold in the public marketplace."

This flaw in the debate reflects a general failing on the part of political scientists. A great deal is known about public opinion at the macrolevel and about decision making at the microlevel. Both have been the focus of extensive research. "We have done rather well . . . on almost every aspect of public opinion *up to* the point where the relationship with policy makers actually begins. But we know strikingly little, in an assured way, about the impact that the body of non-governmental opinion has upon the men who formulate and execute American foreign policy."[9] While this gap remains, the student must rely on plausibility and coherence as tests of contending interpretations. These criteria cannot satisfy anyone who is concerned with the validity of an argument. Failure to specify the linkages condemns us to another sterile and unresolved controversy.

This book seeks to disentangle the manipulation-versus-constraint controversy. It does so by providing an analysis of the linkages between mass opinion and decision making in the concrete setting of three major reorientations in American foreign policy: the shift from isolation and neutrality to alliance and cobelligerence in World War II; the espousal of internationalism in the form of the United Nations Organization; and, finally, the adoption of a bipolar, cold-war orientation. They span a decade that began in 1937 with President Franklin D. Roosevelt's Chicago speech in which he proposed that the aggressor nations be placed in "quarantine." Roosevelt's subsequent retreat from this proposal has come to be regarded as a classic example of the public-opinion *constraint*. The decade closed in 1947 with President Harry S. Truman's speech to a joint session of Congress proposing aid to Greece and Turkey. The Truman Doctrine speech has entered the radical critique not just as the clarion call of the cold war but as a classic example of the *manipu-*

lation of public opinion. The reassessment of these judgments, which is put forward in succeeding chapters, is designed both to shed new light on policy making in these three critical cases and to advance our conceptual understanding of the opinion-policy relationship.

Mobilizing Consent

1

The opinion-policy relationship: An analytic framework

THE OPINION-POLICY RELATIONSHIP

The opinion-policy relationship can be conceived as embodying four elements: public opinion concerning foreign policy; decision making; the transmission of opinion to policy makers; and the diffusion of foreign-policy information to the public.

The first two elements are familiar to most students of foreign policy. Each has been the subject of systematic study for the past twenty-five years at least. A burgeoning literature contains its classics, its revisionist critiques, and its postbehavioral new approaches. The second two elements are less familiar. References to these linkages are dotted throughout the literature, but they are confined to isolated examples or remarks made in passing. Yet without these linkages there would be no opinion-policy relationship but only two discrete phenomena—opinion and policy. The main focus of this book is upon changes in these linkages. By prising open the opinion-policy relationship to reveal its inner workings, we shall be in a better position to evaluate received judgments about the impact of public opinion on foreign policy. In this chapter each of the four elements in the opinion-policy relationship will be considered in turn.

PUBLIC OPINION CONCERNING FOREIGN POLICY

"Any set of ideas, either informational or judgmental, about any aspect of the world scene is considered to constitute a foreign-policy opinion." [10] Arguably, "any aspect of the world scene" is too inclusive, it embraces matters of little or no concern to American policy makers. But an important function of public opinion is to draw such matters into the policy maker's field of vision. This definition has the advantage of not excluding any potentially relevant segment of opinion.

Public opinion concerning foreign policy has generally been treated as a hierarchy. Members of the public are allocated to different strata according to their awareness of foreign-policy issues, their level of information about them, and their capacity to frame coherent opinions. These criteria yield an opinion hierarchy in the form of a pyramid. Its broad base includes the politically oblivious; its narrow apex takes in the policy leadership. Three versions of the pyramid, first drawn up just after World War II, continue to guide contemporary thought: [11]

Kriesberg	Almond	Rosenau
1.	The official policy leadership	
2. The informed	The policy and opinion elites	The opinion makers
3. The aware	The attentive public	The attentive public
4. The unaware	The general public	The mass public

The unaware and the aware but uninformed constitute about 75 percent of the electorate in Martin Kriesberg's analysis. The unaware are ignorant of "almost any given event in American foreign affairs." [12] A slightly larger group is aware of important events but retains little information and cannot frame intelligent arguments about them. These groups correspond with James Rosenau's "mass public" and Gabriel Almond's "general public." "Estimates of its size vary from 75% to 90% of the adult population." [13] "The most predominant mood of the mass public is, of course, indifference and passivity. Except for acute peace-or-war crises (and not always then), the mass public is usually unmoved by the course of world events." [14] This mass is given to mood rather than to structured opinion, to emotion rather than intellect, and to oscillations rather than stability. Rosenau estimates the size of the attentive public at no more than 10 percent of the population, based on the circulation of the quality press.[15] It tends to a more stable pattern of opinion with more structure and depth and so offsets fluctuations in the popular mood. It is inclined toward participation but rarely transcends such amateur steps as joining voluntary organizations or writing to congressmen.

The three sources diverge at the apex of the pyramid. Kriesberg's "the informed" (in line 2) is a nonelite group, part of the corpus of opinion holders, constituting some 25 percent of the electorate. Almond's policy and opinion elite is a narrower stratum, a link in the chain between public and government. He defines it as the "articulate policy-bearing stratum of the population which gives structure to the public and provides the effective means of access to the various groupings."[16] For Rosenau too this stratum is not part of the opinion-holding public but rather an opinion-transmitting linkage. It comprises all those "who occupy positions which enable them regularly to transmit, either locally or nationally, opinions about any issue to unknown persons outside of their occupational field or about more than one class of issues to unknown professional colleagues."[17] It consists of government officials, prominent businessmen, civil servants, journalists, scholars, heads of professional associations, and interest groups. Almond adds a stratum comprising the official policy leadership at the very tip of the pyramid. This group includes the inner circle who regularly participate in the formulation of foreign policy.

The nub of the manipulation-versus-constraint controversy is the role of the mass public. The radical is willing to concede the influence of elite and organized segments of the public with no contest. The traditional scholar, nurtured on the pluralist theory of democracy and mindful of President Eisenhower's warnings about the military-industrial complex, is equally willing to concede the influence of interest groups and the elite.

The debate that this book addresses concerns, primarily, the amorphous body of opinion that is distributed among the general public. The elusiveness of the phenomenon can be gauged by the ways in which parties to the debate describe it; it is "generalized," "nebulous," "superficial," "fickle," and given to "moods."[18] Yet when officials rule out a policy option on the grounds that "the public will not stand for it," it is usually this nebulous entity that they have in mind. Similarly when leaders call for the "wholehearted support of public opinion" as a prerequisite to the success of a policy, the appeal is usually to the general public. The challenge is to discover whether such appeals are mere rhetorical devices, as the radical would have us believe, or whether certain types of decision and certain stages in the policy process are susceptible to the influence of the mass public.

Kriesberg, Almond, and Rosenau helped to identify those segments of the public with opinions of *potential* relevance to foreign policy. Later quantitative studies, using more sophisticated techniques for the secondary analysis of survey data, have not challenged their overall picture of the stratification of opinion.[19] But several caveats and qualifications must be entered before this framework can be adapted to the problem at hand.

First, the sorting of opinion into different strata can only be suggestive. Each level is an abstraction, not a solid stratum as the metaphor from geology implies. The stratification of the foreign-policy public is less well defined and less predictable than in other policy areas, such as labor, transport, agriculture, or resources.[20] The percentages in each level vary across time and between issues. The attentive public expands and contracts, reducing or increasing the remaining ranks of the unaware. In a later work, Rosenau suggests that the attentive public may have expanded in recent years.[21] If true, such a development might be explained by the prominence of Indochina in domestic debate, and by the growth of education and of access to communications.[22]

Second, Rosenau argues that the one major exception to apathy and indifference on the part of the mass public is "an acute peace-or-war crisis." But sustained demand on personal resources also alerts otherwise unaware segments of the general public to foreign-policy issues. The intrusion of foreign policy into everyday life, through conscription, battle casualties, or supplementary taxes, rivets the attention of those normally below the policy-maker's horizon. Conversely a reduced demand on resources or the disappearance of an issue from everyday life can restore the ranks of the indifferent to their full strength. The policy of Vietnamization changed the costs of the Indochina war to the American nation. This secured public acquiescence in unprecedently heavy bombing of North Vietnam in 1972. Robert Tucker comments: "The relative absence of opposition to the war in the last six months of direct American involvement indicated that public—and also, in substantial measure, elite—disaffection with the war had been largely a function of costs (and, of course, the absence of definitive results)."[23]

Third, it is impossible to draw a clear line between opinion-holding members of the public and participants in decision making. Of the three hierarchies, only Kriesberg's is confined to opinion holders. Rosenau and Almond describe a continuum merging into the responsible policy-making elite at the top and the disenfranchised at the bottom. Instead of classifying members of the public in terms of their subjective grasp of foreign-policy information, it is more useful to apply a different test. Morton Halperin measures the influence of members of the bureaucracy upon the president by the probability of their being consulted. [24] A similar test can be extended to public opinion at large to determine the impact of its various groupings on policy. In this extended context, "consultation" should be replaced by "participation." It includes the solicitation of public views and the diffusion of foreign-policy information to the public; for if the decision maker feels obliged to consult or to persuade public opinion, the logical inference is that it holds views he deems relevant to the decision at hand. Not only public-opinion polls, elections, and referenda but also information campaigns preceding a policy initiative constitute "participation." The next section deals with some of the situations in which such participation is likely.

If this alternative method of classifying the opinion-holding public is adopted, the entire foreign-policy process appears as a series of concentric circles. [25] The president and his advisers are at the center; successive circles extend through the bureaucracy and the elite to the attentive and the mass publics. The distance between any circle and the center is not fixed by how well its members are informed but by the probability of their participating in decision making.

DECISION MAKING

This section does not provide a complete decision-making model; rather it pinpoints the types of decisions and the stages in the process at which policy is susceptible to public influence.

By "public influence," we refer primarily to the outer circles of opinion. The inner circles are regularly consulted; their influence has been thoroughly, though not exhaustively, researched and is comparatively uncontroversial.

Indeed, by the mid-1970s intrabureaucratic bargaining had become the dominant paradigm in the study of foreign-policy decision making. [26]

TYPES OF DECISION

Foreign-policy decisions can be ranged on a continuum from "routine" to "unique." "Routine decisions are those where the range of alternatives available to the decision maker is very limited and the criteria for choosing between them are unambiguous. . . . Unique decisions, on the other hand, are those where the range of alternatives is at its maximum and the criteria for choosing between them are unclear or lacking." [27] Unique and routine decisions are categories of the ideal type. In reality, most decisions fall in intermediate positions along the continuum. Sometimes the very nature of a decision enters the political arena. Isolationists believed that once the (unique) decision to pass the 1935 Neutrality Act had been made, decisions concerning when to invoke it would be routine. Internationalists believed that cases such as the undeclared Sino-Japanese war were sufficiently ambiguous to leave several alternatives open. Choosing between these alternatives was then not a routine but a unique decision.

The impact of public opinion on decision making depends on the type of decision. Routine or low-level decisions are usually so unambiguous that reference to any outside opinion is unnecessary. As decisions approach the unique end of the continuum the scope for hesitancy and *in*decision increases. "The greater the uncertainty as to what decision to make, because the alternatives or criteria are unclear, the larger the role which public opinion *can* play in the policy-making process." [28] Whether public opinion *actually* plays its potential role in decision making depends on several other attributes of the situation.

The pressure of time. A crisis decision in which time is of the essence does not permit the canvassing of mass opinion. Only the innermost circles can be consulted. If the president believes that certain options must be evaluated in terms of the likely response of the mass public, members of the inner circle, especially congressional leaders, serve as surrogates. Their estimates of "what the public will stand" are highly subjective.

A less-urgent decision permits time for wider consultation. To a government that has not yet made its decision, the availability of time and the expansion of debate may reinforce a predilection for delay or generate support for the preferred policy alternative.

Encroachment on vested interests. A decision whose outcome touches the interests or sensibilities of potential veto groups is susceptible to public influence. Roosevelt's unwillingness to concede Stalin's known desiderata in Poland before the 1944 elections owed something to the electoral strength of Polish-Americans. [29] In such cases the timing and the content of a decision may be affected by public attitudes.

Intrusion into daily life. Richard Neustadt has observed that the president's constituents outside Washington "only grow attentive when they notice public trouble pressing on their lives." [30] Decisions likely to raise taxes, curtail liberties, bring back the draft, or increase unemployment may require prior public "consultation" to forestall noncompliance or organized protest. As an increasing number of foreign-policy decisions concern wealth and welfare (low policy) and a decreasing number grand strategy (high policy), a greater proportion of decisions can be expected to fall into this category. Decisions whose outcomes do not appear to affect the citizen's daily life are less susceptible to public influence.

Intelligibility of the issue. "Public debate can most easily come to grips with issues which are simple and discrete": [31] to remain neutral in a foreign conflict or to form an alliance; to join an international organization or to remain outside; to pass a bill granting foreign aid or to reject it. In such cases the potential influence of the outer circle of opinion is considerable.

Technical decisions, on the other hand, even those carrying severe budgetary or security implications, generally can be made in seclusion. Most strategic decisions fall into this category. Normally the decision to deploy a new weapons system will remain opaque to the mass public, even if assiduously publicized by I. F. Stone or Jack Anderson. Exceptions occur when parties to the inner debate succeed in going public, by associating the technical decision with some question of widely understood symbolic significance. In the 1930s the most emotive association was "keeping America out of war"; in the 1940s it was "containing communism." In the 1970s an excellent tactic for widening the debate is associating a technical strategic decision with "environmental protection."

Shared images. Decisions in conformity with the dominant climate of opinion [32] require minimum public participation. Decisions that challenge shared images require a wider canvass of opinion. Statesmen in democratic systems often voice the principle that no major departure from the prevailing image of the country's place in world politics should be made without the wholehearted consent of the people. Sometimes this principle is espoused from conviction. Cordell Hull expressed it in his own private notes before the United States decisively rejected isolationism by joining the United Nations. Sometimes it represents a pragmatic decision to invoke mass opinion to stave off dissent from within the elite. This was the case with Harold Wilson's decision to call a referendum on Britain's membership of the European Economic Community in 1975. But mass opinion is more likely to be drawn in, whether for reasons of principle or expediency or both, when the decision threatens shared images of the national experience.

Bargaining. As the previous point suggests, if the inner circle is divided, one or more of the parties may be tempted to widen the debate. In an otherwise even bargaining situation, within the executive or between the executive and the legislature, public opinion can tilt the balance. For this reason congressmen are always suspicious of executive moves to establish direct links with the public over the heads of the legislature. A resourceful bargainer can go public by inspiring a leak or by publicizing the results of opinion polls that support his preferred outcome. Some government agencies are in a position to commission their own polls and to release their results selectively. The probability of mass involvement, precipitated by these or other stratagems, depends on the degree of consensus among members of the inner circle, their comparative bargaining strength, and their ability to evoke expressions of popular sentiment.

The different attributes of a situation considered above are overlapping. One aspect of a decision may point in the direction of a wide-ranging canvass of opinion; another aspect may suggest a choice made in seclusion. For example, it may be necessary to make a decision that shatters shared images under the pressure of time; a unique decision, with far-reaching implications for daily life, may be made in a technical area. It is, therefore, the overall configuration of these attributes that determines whether public involvement will be triggered in any specific situation.

STAGES IN DECISION MAKING

Political scientists have long recognized that foreign-policy decision making is a multistage process.[33] This recognition is particularly important in situations where the president or secretary of state appears to dominate the process, for, in such cases, scholars are tempted to reduce the problem to one of personality. But even the most self-reliant chief executive is subject to constraints. By breaking down the decision process we can pinpoint the stages at which the impact of public opinion can be felt:

a. Identification of the issue.
b. Specification of policy options.
c. Selection of desired policy.
d. Implementation.

Identification of the issue. Certain kinds of international events are so salient that they ineluctably present themselves to the policy maker for decision; spectacular acts of aggression against allies or friendly states, the seizure of a naval or merchant vessel in peacetime are prime examples. But even in these situations the climate of opinion can affect the timing of a decision. In the 1930s Axis aggression was not accepted as an issue requiring an American decision for several years. In the 1940s communist aggression was identified as an issue requiring a definite decision far more rapidly. The intervening experience of war had imprinted "the lessons of appeasement" on an entire generation, hastening the identification of the issue.

In less spectacular cases an issue may never be identified as one requiring an American decision unless it is brought to the attention of policy makers by concerned segments of opinion. It is more likely to be in-house opinion, if the issue is technical, if it does not encroach on vested interests, or if it does not impinge on daily life. It is more likely to be external opinion if the issue is nontechnical or if the other conditions for public involvement are satisfied. Sometimes an issue will be raised by key members of the inner circle acting as spokesmen or surrogates for outside constituencies. External events are only one source of stimulation for foreign-policy decisions. "Most decisions are responses to domestic pressures, and the actions of other nations often figure merely as devices for argument."[34]

Specification of policy options. Once an issue has been identified, the universe of possible policy alternatives must be narrowed to those that are feasible. Feasibility depends on political, economic, and technical conditions but also on the opinion environment.[35] An option may not be feasible if it carries with it the threat of a veto or of reprisals (e.g., at the ballot) from affected segments of the public or if it clashes with shared images. In situations requiring an immediate decision, the limits of public tolerance can only be assessed subjectively, if at all. But in decisions where time is not crucial, it is often possible to determine the limits of popular tolerance more precisely.

In addition to the pressure of time—and the other attributes of a decision enumerated in the previous section—the probability of the participation of mass opinion depends on its accessibility. Before the advent of opinion polls, the president had to rely on his own intuition and the advocacy of surrogates if he wished to assess the feasibility of a policy in terms of public attitudes. This enabled him to reject options on the nonfalsifiable grounds that "the public would not stand for it." Opinion polls and their transmission on the inner circle provided an alternative and more direct "vox populi." This made it more difficult, though by no means impossible, to rule out an option by projecting one's own preferences onto unaggregated and unarticulated mass opinion.

Selection of desired policy. Having identified the issue and reviewed the set of feasible options, policy makers must choose their preferred course of action. The actual decision is also a potential target for public opinion. The ideal decision commands immediate support from all segments of opinion. Because most decisions are anything but ideal in this respect, the policy maker must make accommodations and trade-offs. His prime concern will be to identify potential veto groups. Their support must be safeguarded even at the cost of verbal or substantive concessions. But the opinions of those sections of the public that do not possess a veto or that are likely to prove intractable may be dispensed with. This was Roosevelt's final course with respect to diehard isolationists between 1939 and 1941.

Often a president's own penchant for delay or a logjam caused by disagreement among his advisers can postpone a decision. If the president himself favors delay, selective inattention may lead him to pick up only those expressions of opinion that support further postponement. This was Roosevelt's reaction to the public response to his quarantine speech in 1937. A decision not to decide may be tempting when claims of equal merit are made to the same scarce resources. This situation is common between different branches of the armed forces. If an issue has been swept under the carpet, an intense and concerted public opinion can force resolution. Because such expressions of opinion rarely occur spontaneously, it is up to those members of the inner circle favoring resolution to elicit public support.

Implementation. Between decision and action there is ample scope for a policy to miscarry. Public opinion is one of the elements that may intervene to determine whether implementation actually occurs. This is particularly true in a system where an executive decision must be underwritten financially by an independent legislature before it can be implemented.

Consider a case in which the executive has made a decision in principle. For this principle to be implemented, legislative endorsement and appropriations are required. Such endorsement will be forthcoming only if it appears prudent to key congressional leaders. One of the components of legislative prudence is constituent opinion, which is crystallized in several forms: group representations, congressional mail, editorial opinion, private or commercial opinion surveys, and, more traditionally, the political instinct of the politician. [36]

Implementation, then, may await the articulation of opinion by relevant publics. If a definite public verdict is not articulated spontaneously or extracted by the polls, implementation may await the mobilization of public consent. Indeed legislators may insist that the executive itself engage in the mobilization of consent as a condition of legislative approval. This was the case with the decision to establish the United Nations and with the Truman plan for aid to Greece and Turkey; the government organized large-scale foreign policy information programs to mobilize consent for both these policy innovations.

In other cases, the public mood or its congressional emanation can intervene to prevent a decision being implemented. Following the Paris Peace accords of December 1973, President Richard Nixon and Dr. Henry Kissinger decided it was necessary to continue aid to South Vietnam if the Thieu regime were to survive. But public opinion ran against such support so Congress voted to withhold further appropriations. This led to a quick depletion in spare parts and other back-up supplies for the South Vietnamese military forces and their eventual capitulation in May 1975. On this occasion public opinion intervened to prevent the implementation of a major foreign-policy decision. [37]

Another opportunity for the intervention of public opinion between decision and action is provided by the administrative personnel. "Rarely does the decision maker implement the policy decision which he has made; he makes decisions which others implement. The separation of the process into decisional and implementational components means that the contents of a policy decision may be drastically altered at the implementation stage."[38] Harry Truman thought the most chastening experience for a new president was to give orders to do this or that and to find that nothing would happen.[39]

Sometimes a decision is made by one department but must be implemented by another. If the two branches have different public constituencies and their interests clash, implementation may be delayed. An example of this occurred during the October 1973 Middle East war. If the semiofficial version of these events can be accepted,[40] an early decision by the secretary of state to undertake immediate resupply of the Israel Defense Forces was not implemented at once by the Department of Defense. Only the insistence of the president compelled compliance by the Pentagon. One reason for noncompliance, it is suggested, was the susceptibility of the secretary of defense to the oil lobby, while the White House was closer to supporters of Israel in the Congress and among the public. This type of intervention is most likely in situations where branches of the bureaucracy have their own sectional constituents with limited objectives.

LINKAGES

The previous section noted the types of decision and the stages in decision making where opportunities exist for the intervention of public opinion. But the identification of such opportunities tells us little about the specific linkages between what the public believes and how decision makers behave. Of course, polls appearing in the press form part of the policy maker's diet of news. But we simply do not know whether this kind of "extracted" opinion has any impact at all on decisions.

In order to find out more about this impact we can conceptualize the linkages between opinion and policy by extending two functional categories used in the old public-affairs office of the State Department: the intelligence function and the information function.[41] The former refers to the process of gathering, analyzing, and transmitting public-opinion data to officials responsible for policy decisions. The latter refers to the diffusion of information concerning foreign policy to the public. In wartime the information function overlaps with domestic propaganda work.

The two processes are less independent than this functional division suggests. First, the same agencies are often responsible for both. Second, the impact of public opinion on policy makers is affected by the proficiency of the apparatus available for getting the government's view across. A working hypothesis of this book is that *the more highly developed the government's information function, the weaker the public opinion constraint appears to be.*

The following outline of the two linkages between opinion and policy contains fewer empirical generalizations than earlier sections of this chapter. The discussion is cast more in terms of questions than of answers. These questions pose the basic research task to which later chapters are a response.

THE TRANSMISSION OF OPINION TO POLICY MAKERS

This rubric replaces the more limited "intelligence function" that the State Department used during the 1940s. As an amorphous set of attitudes distributed among the population, public opinion is neither accessible nor germane to the foreign-policy process. It can enter the process only when crystallized, articulated, and "submitted" to those involved in the formulation of policy. [42] Mass opinion is crystallized most tangibly in public-opinion polls. Unlike nonextracted sources of mass opinion, the polls make some claim to tap the mysterious substrata of otherwise inarticulate opinion.

Commercial and private opinion polls were introduced during the 1930s. Like the policy makers of the time, the modern researcher has access to several series of polls on foreign-policy themes. The first step in assessing their impact on policy is to establish whether their findings reached the inner circle. Fortunately details of the transmission of poll data are preserved in official correspondence and memoranda. One of the advantages of analyzing decisions made several decades ago is the availability of written evidence. The choice of questions in polls specially commissioned by government agencies is another clue to the kind of data that actually penetrated the policy process.

But even if we succeed in delineating the transmission channels and their content we return to the problem of official perceptions. Were the reports and opinions digests read? If read were they regarded with confidence or skepticism? The magnitude of the problem facing the researcher is suggested by Stephen Early, President Roosevelt's press secretary, in his reply to an enquiry from Wilson Doyle of the University of Alabama. Doyle had been engaged in an evaluation of the Gallup and Fortune polls and wished to know whether the president consulted them regularly and, if so, how accurate and authoritative he considered them to be. Early replied that

> the President in the course of his reading at one time or another sees most of the important polls. I regret, however, that the course he has pursued ever since he has been in the White House prevents me from giving you any expression of opinion concerning the value the President attaches to them. [43]

Although evasive, this letter does contain some useful information. It was written only six years after the establishment of the Gallup poll, in the days before presidents had become famous for assailing visitors with pockets full of polls. The extent to which the polls had already become required presidential reading is, therefore, rather surprising. Early's reluctance to go into details can be attributed in part to considerations of fair commerce. In transmitting poll results to the White House, Hadley Cantril of the Office of Public Opinion Research at Princeton often stressed the need for confidentiality, especially with prepublication Gallup data. Relations between Cantril, a Roosevelt partisan, and Cantril's business and academic colleagues might have been seriously jeopardized if the president's privileged access to survey findings had become generally known.

The establishment or dissolution of opinion-gathering agencies was often the occasion for statements concerning their utility. A retiring agency head could speak far more freely than an incumbent and might have been motivated to do so by the circumstances of his departure. Elmer Davis, for example, wrote a long and revealing report to the president on his retirement as head of the Office of War Information. [44] Requests to the Congress for appropriations to pay for opinion surveys were often accompanied by testimony that explained their place in policy making. Legislators generally believed that a direct government line to vox populi threatened their prerogatives. This conviction eventually led to the curtailment of the State Department's polling operation in 1957.

Finally, having determined when and how public opinion enters the foreign-policy process, a crucial political question remains: the capacity of the opinion holders to act as a veto group. A veto can be exercised through congressional intermediaries, the threat of electoral censure, strikes, or other sources of political embarrassment.[45] But these potential constraints are routine features of political life; their particular importance depends on the official's vulnerability to public opinion. A generalized belief in the need for public support, coupled with a predisposition toward action or inaction, can form a filter for the acceptance or rejection of specific opinions.

THE DIFFUSION OF FOREIGN-POLICY INFORMATION TO THE PUBLIC

The marketing metaphor is such a ubiquitous feature of contemporary political analysis that we often forget its comparatively recent advent. Of course, it has been necessary to "sell" candidates to the electorate ever since the establishment of democracy. With the expansion of the suffrage and of mass communications, the "selling" of candidates and their domestic policies has proceeded apace. But foreign policy, traditionally the prerogative of the diplomatic specialist, is a comparative newcomer to public relations. Perhaps inhibited by the constitutional powers of Congress in this area, even presidents who were most adept at direct appeals to the public on domestic matters hesitated to exploit their potential as opinion makers in foreign affairs.[46]

Wars provide the major exception to this diffidence. Woodrow Wilson seized the initiative during World War I and set up an elaborate mechanism for getting his views on war aims and the postwar settlement across to the American people. But congressional suspicions of partisan motives prevented the machinery for such direct communications with the public from surviving into peacetime.[47] Franklin Roosevelt created links with the public on an unprecedented scale during the 1930s, but they were confined to domestic matters. No attempt was made to "sell" a more vigilant foreign policy as the New Deal legislation had been sold. Only the German invasion of Poland and Britain's declaration of war persuaded Roosevelt and his advisers to mobilize public opinion for repeal of the arms embargo provisions of the Neutrality Act.

The war not only imprinted a counter appeasement image in the minds of policy makers; it also taught them how to elicit public acceptance for such an image. The German experience created both a transferable negative concept—totalitarianism—and the apparatus needed to mobilize consent for a more active American role in world politics. Wartime experience in the management of foreign-policy information and the manipulation of symbols was put to effective use in the campaign for American sponsorship of the United Nations Organization and for the Truman Doctrine. Thereafter it became almost a reflex for the executive to mount an information campaign whenever a foreign-policy decision was contemplated which met the conditions for the intervention of public opinion specified earlier in this chapter. The "packaging and selling" of foreign policy was seen in the Marshall Plan, the Korean War, the New Look, and the Indochina war, to name only the most manifest examples. [48] Publication of the Pentagon Papers, the Watergate case, and America's thinly disguised defeat in Indochina may have checked the executive's ability to mobilize consent for its foreign policy by means of marketing techniques.

The development of a foreign-affairs information machine does not necessarily corroborate the radical view that public opinion imposes no constraints on foreign policy. The very need to mobilize consent often leads to modifications in policy before a definite decision is reached. Public-opinion polls tax the credibility of members of the inner circle as surrogates for the general public. Finally, the public is not a passive recipient of government propaganda. Its apathy and indifference cannot be taken for granted, especially when foreign-policy issues intrude into daily life. Without anticipating the conclusions of later chapters, it is a fair assumption that neither the constraint nor the manipulation model is fully supported by the data: "Just as it would be naive to accept the traditional civics-book view that the managers of American foreign policy are responding to the desires of the American public, instead of shaping those desires, it would be equally misleading to conclude that the public has no influence or that it is indefinitely 'educable.'" [49]

A HISTORICAL OVERVIEW

The years between 1937 and 1947 were selected for several reasons. First, they witnessed three shifts in the dominant foreign-policy orientation of the United States. These shifts marked a rapid transition from the relatively stable isolationism of the two preceding decades to the relatively stable cold-war orientation of the two succeeding ones. [50]

1. The Japanese attack on Pearl Harbor transformed an already decaying isolationism into alliance and cobelligerence with Britain and the Soviet Union.

2. This alliance formed the core of a new type of American internationalism designed to build a system of collective security around the victorious coalition.

3. But Soviet-American cooperation did not long survive the defeat of the Axis. The restrained hostility that replaced it became the pivot of international relations and the dominant element in American foreign policy. It produced a bipolar international system and a cold war orientation in foreign policy whose principal public text is the Truman Doctrine speech of March 12, 1947.

A second reason for selecting the period between 1937 and 1947 is suggested by two presidential addresses, one at either end of the decade; Roosevelt's quarantine speech and Truman's speech recommending aid to Greece and Turkey. These speeches point to the changed configuration of the international system; they signal the transition from isolationism to activism in American foreign policy; and they have been called classic examples of the public-opinion constraint on the one hand and the power of manipulation on the other.

Third, the tensions produced by these realignments provide unusual opportunities to study the opinion-policy relationship. Alliance partners and enemies changed dramatically between 1937 and 1947, placing severe strains on shared images of the United States' place in world politics. These changes both challenged and evoked unusually explicit statements of conventional assumptions about the appropriate role for public opinion in the formulation of a democratic foreign policy.

Fourth, the impact of war transformed the machinery available to the foreign-policy bureaucracy for analyzing and transmitting public opinion to high-level decision makers. In 1937 virtually no institutionalized procedures existed for this purpose, and there were no branches of the bureaucracy specifically charged with mobilizing popular support for government initiatives. A succession of wartime emergency agencies developed techniques for submitting opinion to policy makers and for diffusing foreign-policy information to the public. These techniques, and many of the personnel responsibile for them, were inherited by existing federal departments, notably the Department of State.

VERNON REGIONAL
JUNIOR COLLEGE LIBRARY

The period between 1944 and 1947 was the heyday of the Office of Public Affairs at State. In the campaign to mobilize support for American participation in the United Nations Organization, public-affairs operations played a critical role. By 1947, when, in recognition of new international realities, the United States adopted a more "selective" approach to security, a new foreign-policy information program was almost a reflex reaction. Such campaigns were keyed to the condition of public attitudes revealed by the department's "American Opinion Reports," which were distributed to foreign service and Washington officials. Public-information specialists played an unprecedented role in the formulation of policy in the weeks before President Truman proposed American assistance to Greece and Turkey.

A final reason for selecting the years between 1937 and 1947 concerns the availability of data. This period is sufficiently distant to permit access to once secret government documents, including confidential reports on public opinion and internal memorandums on public information campaigns.

The remainder of this chapter will provide an overview of historical judgments about the opinion-policy relationship in each of the three major shifts in foreign policy indicated above. In each case we shall elicit the assumptions underlying historians' interpretation of events. Then, in later chapters, data gathered for the present study will be used to evaluate these assumptions and to suggest alternatives.

ISOLATIONISM

"The United States position in regard to foreign affairs is determined by American public opinion, on which the President and Congress are dependent."[51] So German Ambassador Hans Heinrich Dieckhoff reported to the head of the Political Section of the German Foreign Office on December 20, 1937. It followed that a potential adversary, or student of international politics, would do well to examine the condition of public opinion if he wished to predict shifts in American foreign policy. The predominance of the isolationists would last until Americans realized the incompatibility of their position with the survival of liberalism and democracy in Europe; then "the jump from a policy of isolation to one of intervention will not be very great."[52]

Dieckhoff's analysis has been endorsed by a generation of scholars who argue that Roosevelt's impulse to intercede against Axis aggression was checked by the dead weight of domestic isolationism.[53] American foreign policy became more active only when part of this weight had been lifted. James MacGregor Burns is struck by the unresponsiveness of American opinion to events in Europe and Asia. "Each time in the race between aggression and American opinion victory went to the former."[54] Foreign-policy decisions, he argues, responded even more slowly since the president "tagged along with opinion" or even lagged behind it, always exaggerating critical elements in the response to his proposals.

Robert Divine does not discern a frustrated interventionist impulse beneath the policy of neutrality. Until the collapse of the Munich agreement in 1939, the policy leadership, including the president, shared the isolationist ethos prevailing among the general public. Even when the president decided to back away from isolationism and neutrality he "acted only after the interventionists had created strong public support," as in the case of the destroyers-for-bases deal with Britain and the eventual decision to send convoys into the Atlantic. Always a close student of the polls, "the President would rather follow public opinion than lead it."[55]

This argument is bolstered by evidence of Roosevelt's sensitivity to the polls, a commercial innovation introduced during his first administration. "He watched the fledgling polls carefully," writes Lloyd Free, "and above all followed with avid interest data especially collected by my late colleague Hadley Cantril, charting trends in American opinion in connection with the war. With a close eye on Cantril's data, Roosevelt paced his course, escalating his effort to aid the British and defeat the Axis step by gradual step."[56]

Some argue that Roosevelt's natural caution and political prudence pointed to a policy of appeasement. With rare exceptions, such as the quarantine speech, the president was not a man to go out on a limb to proclaim a controversial policy. Donald Watt argues that his personal sensitivities were reinforced by Cordell Hull and Sumner Welles "with their renewed concerns for American isolationist opinion."[57]

In order to substantiate the charge of "appeasement," it would be necessary to argue that the president could have mobilized opinion against the Axis faster than he did—that is, to demonstrate that there were prerogatives available to the government in its role as opinion maker that were neglected and that public opinion was less resolutely isolationist and, hence, less of a constraint than statesmen and scholars have maintained.

So the persistence of isolationism in the teeth of spectacular aggression in Europe and the Far East has, in large part, been laid at the door of public opinion. Those scholars who believe that Roosevelt reached an "early" decision to resist the Axis suggest that public opinion intervened to prevent implementation of the decision. Those scholars who, like Divine, believe that the president and his advisers shared the isolationist ethos until a later date suggest that public opinion intervened to delay the decision itself. Both of these interpretations share the German ambassador's assumption that in the United States foreign policy was a function of domestic opinion and that the government's role as opinion maker was negligible. Popular rejection of Roosevelt's quarantine proposal has become the classic example of a public-opinion constraint.

INTERNATIONALISM

The establishment of the United Nations Organization is another case in which the opinion-policy relationship was important. John Lewis Gaddis takes up the theme of the president's sensitivity to public opinion. "Painfully aware of Wilson's experience with the Senate," he writes, "chronically prone to exaggerate domestic opposition to his foreign policy, Roosevelt hesitated to declare himself publicly in favor of a new collective security agency."[58] Nevertheless, observing the successful agitation of internationalist groups, he permitted the State Department to go ahead with plans for the United Nations. Gradually the president allowed his own internationalism to emerge, while Cordell Hull secured Soviet approval in Moscow in 1943 and at Dumbarton Oaks in 1944.

Having committed the country to the idea of the United Nations in international negotiations, policy makers viewed the problem as one of neutralizing possible opposition from isolationist elements in the Congress and elsewhere. To this end the State Department mounted its own U.N. campaign, the culmination of a decade of agitation by private and semiprivate groups. By 1944 public-opinion polls showed general acceptance of American participation in the world organization but Roosevelt, wanted to make sure. Some senators were nervous about such a major departure from American practice and sought guarantees of public support. Edward R. Stettinius, Cordell Hull's under-secretary and later secretary of state, launched a large-scale public-relations campaign, strengthening public affairs machinery in the State Department and making novel use of movies and radio. The government's success in mobilizing public support was symbolized by the presence of "consultants" representing forty-two citizen groups at the San Francisco conference. [59]

Robert Riggs questions the "myth" that the U.N. charter was "oversold" to the American people. [60] He agrees that a "vigorous selling campaign was unquestionably conducted" but disputes the argument that the content of this campaign encouraged millennial expectations. Publicity material left no doubt that the active cooperation of all the great powers was a prerequisite for the U.N.'s success. But he accepts the observation that "a veritable wave of propaganda and influence was generated on behalf of American membership." [61]

In this instance the implicit model of the opinion-policy relationship is more complex. Although collective security had gained early recognition by policy makers as an issue for decision, it was only fully accepted by them after segments of the attentive public and the opinion elites had generated widespread support. Once the leaders had made their favorable decision they adopted the role of opinion makers to mobilize consent for implementation. Because American membership in the United Nations was a radical departure from its aloofness toward the League of Nations a thoroughgoing shift in attitudes was required. The government's informational activities were, therefore, aimed at targets throughout the hierarchy of public opinion.

THE TRUMAN DOCTRINE

The decision for the United States to replace Britain as the economic and military guarantor of the Greek and Turkish governments involved the country in a reorientation of its foreign policy that was probably more fundamental than that symbolized by its adherence to the U.N. charter. "For the first time in its history," Stephen Ambrose writes, "the United States had chosen to intervene in a period of general peace in the affairs of people outside of North and South America." [62] The plan required an immediate appropriation of $400 million, a large claim on a Republican Congress that had so recently been persuaded of the need for multilateral collective security. Senator Arthur Vandenberg of Michigan, the republican chairman of the Senate Foreign Relations Committee made his vital support conditional upon the administration's exerting itself to mobilize domestic opinion. This it did both in Truman's speech to a joint session of Congress on March 12, 1947, and in the accompanying public information program, which was organized by a subcommittee of the State-War-Navy Coordinating Committee. The main lines of the subcommittee's program were:

> To make possible the formulation of intelligent opinions by the American people on the problems created by the present situation in Greece through the furnishing of full and frank information by the government.
> To portray the world conflict between free and totalitarian or imposed forms of government.
> To bring about an understanding by the American people of the world strategic situation.[63]

The Office of Public Affairs at the State Department conducted thorough analyses of the public's response in an effort to identify and neutralize potential criticisms. Ironically the major source of criticism was the neglect of the United Nations. Jones observes that within a week of the president's speech "the overwhelming attachment of the American public to the United Nations made itself felt in no uncertain terms." For the majority of the public "the United Nations in the first two years of its existence had become the halfway house on the road from isolationism to full responsibility in world affairs, and they were uncritically sold on it." There was some public oposition, but it was muted. Bipartisan congressional majorities approved appropriations to finance aid to Greece and Turkey and, later, the more ambitious Marshall Plan.

Summarizing the oscillations in the opinion-policy relationship at this time, Gaddis suggests that public attitudes toward the U.S.S.R. had pushed the administration toward a policy of confrontation but that the government, in turn, had to jolt public and congressional opinion in order to extract the necessary financial backing. "The Truman Doctrine constituted a form of shock therapy: it was a last ditch effort by the Administration to prod Congress and the American people into accepting the responsibilities of world leadership which, one year earlier, largely in response to public opinion, Washington officials had assumed by deciding to 'get tough with Russia.'"[64]

In this case the opinion-policy relationship is conceived as a two-way process, but one in which the diffusion of information to the public was more significant than the transmission of public opinion to the government. Of the three reorientations surveyed in this chapter the decision to replace Britain in the Mediterranean region was the one in which the government acted most decisively as opinion maker.

The revisionist view of the mobilization function of the Truman Doctrine differs from that of insiders, like Joseph Jones, and more orthodox scholars, like Gaddis, in its cynicism. The problem was not "how to reflect public opinion, or even to change it, but how to overcome its potentially negative consequences. And for this, ultimately, nothing was superior to a world crisis, real or fancied, and conjuring up the menace of Russia and Communism."[65] The issues involved in aid to Greece and Turkey were deliberately distorted in order to launch a global crusade against forces of national liberation. As such, the revisionist argues, the Truman Doctrine is a classic example of the *manipulation* of public opinion in support of predetermined policy choices.

NOTES

1. The point which this debate has reached may be judged by consulting Robert James Maddox, *The New Left and the Origins of the Cold War* (Princeton, 1973). This work is exclusively devoted to discrediting the scholarship of those historians with whose conclusions the author disagrees. It is in the spirit of this debate that no attempt is made to correct the errors of those scholars with whose conclusions the author agrees. For the inevitable rejoinders see *The New York Times Book Review,* June 17, 1973, and Ronald Steel's critique in *The New York Review of Books,* June 14, 1973.
2. John Lewis Gaddis, *The United States and the Origins of the Cold War, 1941-1947* (New York, 1972), contains a subtle analysis of the interplay between domestic and international considerations in the preoccupations of foreign-policy makers.
3. J. David Singer, "The Level-of-Analysis Problem in International Relations," in J. N. Rosenau, ed., *International Politics and Foreign Policy* (New York, 1969), p. 27.
4. James Bryce, *Modern Democracies* (New York, 1921), chap. 62. See also Bernard Berelson, "Democratic Theory and Public Opinion," *Public Opinion Quarterly* (Fall 1952).
5. Thomas A. Bailey, *The Man in the Street: The Impact of American Public Opinion on Foreign Policy* (New York, 1948), p. 10.
6. Walter Lippmann, *The Public Philosophy* (Boston, 1955), p. 19.
7. Theodore Sorensen, *Decision-Making in the White House* (New York, 1963), p. 46.
8. Joyce Kolko and Gabriel Kolko, *The Limits of Power: The World and United States Foreign Policy* (New York, 1972), p. 333.
9. Bernard C. Cohen, "The Relationship between Public Opinion and Foreign Policy Maker," in Melvin Small, ed., *Public Opinion and Historians* (Detroit, 1970), p. 66.
10. J. N. Rosenau, *Public Opinion and Foreign Policy* (New York, 1961), p. 16.
11. Martin Kriesberg, "Dark Areas of Ignorance," in Lester Markel, ed., *Public Opinion and Foreign Policy* (New York, 1949), pp. 51-52; Gabriel Almond, *The American*

People and Foreign Policy (New York, 1950), p. 138; Rosenau, *Public Opinion and Foreign Policy*, pp. 35-41.

12. Kriesberg, "Dark Areas of Ignorance," pp. 49-52.

13. Rosenau, *Public Opinion and Foreign Policy*, pp. 35-39.

14. Ibid.

15. Ibid.

16. Almond, *The American People*, p. 138.

17. Rosenau, *Public Opinion and Foreign Policy*, pp. 34-35.

18. Gabriel Almond is largely responsible for the conception of foreign-policy opinion in terms of "mood." See his *The American People*. For a critique of "The Mood Theory," see William R. Caspary, *American Political Science Review* (June 1970).

19. See, for example, John E. Mueller, *War, Presidents and Public Opinion* (New York, 1973).

20. Samuel P. Huntington, *The Common Defense* (New York, 1961), p. 178; Bernard C. Cohen, *The Public's Impact on Foreign Policy* (Boston, 1973), pp. 78-79.

21. James N. Rosenau, *The Attentive Public and Foreign Policy: A Theory of Growth and Some New Evidence*, Research Monograph 31, Center for International Studies (Princeton, 1968).

22. Mueller, *War*, p. 164.

23. Robert W. Tucker, "Vietnam: The Final Reckoning," *Commentary* (May 1975): 31; see also his "The American Outlook: Change and Continuity," in Tucker et al., *Retreat from Empire?* (Baltimore, 1973), p. 36.

24. Morton H. Halperin, *Bureaucratic Politics and Foreign Policy* (Washington D.C., 1974), pp. 17-18.

25. Roger Hilsman, *To Move a Nation* (Garden City, New York, 1967), p. 542.

26. See Richard Neustadt, *Alliance Politics* (New York, 1970); Graham T. Allison, *Essence of Decision: Explaining the Cuban Missile Crisis* (Boston, 1971); Graham T. Allison and Morton H. Halperin, "Bureaucratic Politics: A Paradigm and Some Policy Implications," in Raymond Tanter and Richard H. Ullman, eds., *Theory and Policy in International Relations* (Princeton, 1972); Morton H. Halperin and Arnold Kanter, *Readings in American Foreign Policy: A Bureaucratic Perspective* (Boston, 1973); and Halperin, *Bureaucratic Politics and Foreign Policy*.

27. James J. Best, *Public Opinion, Micro and Macro* (Homewood, Illinois, 1973), p. 219.

28. Ibid., p. 222.

29. Stalin, of course, understood that Western statesmen would claim varying degrees of thralldom to public opinion depending on their bargaining position. At the Teheran conference Roosevelt told Stalin that he could not publicly endorse Soviet incorporation of the Baltic states since American public opinion would demand referenda and observance of the principle of self-determination. Stalin politely suggested that FDR undertake some propaganda work at home. Gaddis, *The United States*, p. 139. This is a specific example of the advantage that can generally be secured in international negotiations by arguing that one cannot make certain concessions because of public opinion at home. It often pays negotiators to make "statements calculated to arouse a public opinion that permits no concessions to be made" before engaging in negotiations. Thomas C. Schelling, *The Strategy of Conflict* (Oxford, 1970), p. 28.

30. Richard E. Neustadt, *Presidential Power: The Politics of Leadership* (New York, 1960), pp. 99-100.

31. Huntington, *The Common Defense*, p. 177.

32. Warner R. Schilling, "The Politics of National Defense: Fiscal 1950," in Warner R. Schilling, Paul Y. Hammond, and Glenn H. Snyder, *Strategy, Politics and Defense Budgets* (New York, 1962), pp. 97-98.

33. See, for example, Richard C. Snyder, H. W. Bruck, and Burton Sapin, eds., *Foreign Policy Decision-Making: An Approach to the Study of International Politics* (New York, 1962).

34. Halperin, *Bureaucratic Politics*, p. 102.

35. Best, *Public Opinion*, p. 229.

36. Martin Kriesberg, "What Congressmen and Administrators Think of the Polls," *Public Opinion Quarterly* (Fall 1945); Lewis Anthony Dexter, "What Do Congressmen Hear: The Mail," *Public Opinion Quarterly* (Spring 1956).

37. "There was never any proposition that the United States would withdraw and cut off aid, and these agreements were negotiated on the assumption that the United States would continue economic and military aid to South Vietnam." Henry Kissinger, press conference, Department of State, March 26, 1975.

38. Best, *Public Opinion*, p. 247.

39. Neustadt, *Presidential Power*, p. 22.

40. The semiofficial version is contained in Marvin Kalb and Bernard Kalb, *Kissinger* (London, 1974), pp. 450-478. The Kalbs are understood to have had the close coopera-tion of the secretary of state in preparing their book. Their version of these events is challenged in Edward N. Luttwak and Walter Laqueur, "Kissinger and the Yom Kippur War," *Commentary* (September 1974).

41. Lester Markel, "Opinion a Neglected Instrument," in Markel et al., *Public Opinion and Foreign Policy*, pp. 29-33.

42. Rosenau, *Public Opinion and Foreign Policy*, pp. 19-26.

43. Early to Doyle, October 7, 1941, Official File, Box 857, Franklin D. Roosevelt Library, Hyde Park, New York.

44. "Report to the President, 1942-1945," Papers of Elmer Davis, OWI Subject File, Box 10, Library of Congress.

45. Kenneth N. Waltz, "Electoral Punishment and Foreign Policy Crises," in James N. Rosenau, ed., *Domestic Sources of Foreign Policy* (New York, 1967).

46. Elmer E. Cornwell Jr., *Presidential Leadership of Public Opinion* (Bloomington, Indiana, 1965), chap. 6; Arthur M. Schlesinger, Jr., *The Imperial Presidency* (New York, 1974), pp. 96-99.

47. For details see chapter 3.

48. Theodore J. Lowi, "Making Democracy Safe for the World: National Politics and Foreign Policy," in Rosenau, ed., *Domestic Sources*.

49. Richard Barnet, *Roots of War: The Men and Institutions Behind U.S. Foreign Policy* (Baltimore, 1971), p. 242.

50. "Isolationism" is a term fraught with controversy. It is used here not to denote com-plete isolation (economic autarky and withdrawal from diplomatic relations); rather it refers to the goal of preserving "the American government's absolute control over its

foreign policy by avoiding any long term political commitments, either actual or implied, to other nations." Manfred Jonas, *Isolationism in America, 1935-1941* (Ithaca, 1966), p. 5.

51. Dieckhoff to von Weissacker, December 20, 1937, translated by Manfred Jonas and cited by Jonas, *Isolationism*, p. 209.

52. Dieckhoff to Foreign Office (Berlin), October 9, 15, 1937, in Jonas, *Isolationism*, p. 208.

53. Some dissent from this interpretation is noted in chapter 2.

54. James MacGregor Burns, *Roosevelt: The Lion and the Fox* (New York, 1956).

55. The remark was attributed to Harry Hopkins by Henry Morgenthau. John M. Blum, *From the Morgenthau Diaries* (Boston, 1959), pp. 253-254, cited by Robert A. Divine, *Roosevelt and World War II* (Baltimore, 1969), p. 42.

56. Lloyd A. Free, "The Introversion-Extroversion Cycle in National Mood in Recent Decades," prepared for delivery at the annual conference of the American Association for Public Opinion Research, May 18, 1973.

57. Donald Watt, "Roosevelt and Chamberlain, Two Appeasers," *International Journal* (Spring 1973).

58. Gaddis, *The United States and the Origins of the Cold War*, p. 25.

59. John Sloan Dickey, "The Secretary and the American Public," in Don Price, ed., *The Secretary of State* (Englewood Cliffs, 1960), pp. 146-147.

60. Robert E. Riggs, "Overselling the U.N. Charter—Fact and Myth," *International Organization* 14 (Spring 1960).

61. Richard C. Snyder and Edgar S. Furniss Jr., *American Foreign Policy* (New York, 1954), p. 793.

62. Stephen E. Ambrose, *Rise to Globalism: American Foreign Policy, 1938-1970* (Baltimore, 1971), p. 152.

63. Cited by Joseph M. Jones, *The Fifteen Weeks* (New York, 1955), p. 152.

64. Gaddis, *The United States and the Origins of the Cold War*, p. 351.

65. Kolko and Kolko, *The Limits of Power*, p. 334.

2

The public opinion constraint: A classic example?

If the Truman Doctrine has been viewed by historians as a classic case of the *manipulation* of public opinion, Roosevelt's retreat from his proposal to quarantine the aggressor nations has been viewed as a classic example of the public opinion *constraint*. Of course the situations were not symmetrical. The experience of war had taught certain lessons. The appeasement analogy taught that aggression must always be nipped in the bud. This helps to explain Truman's rapid success in linking American national interests with events in far-away countries of which the American people still knew very little. Another lesson was contained in the concept of totalitarianism. Totalitarian dictators had to be treated differently: their word, whether at Munich or Yalta, was not their bond.

Other comparisons between the situations in 1937 and 1947 refer to differences in the leadership styles of Roosevelt and Truman and to the altered balance between the executive and the legislature. In the 1930s Roosevelt tried to bring neutrality legislation more into line with his preferences, but he did not challenge the right of Congress to set the main lines of the country's foreign policy. In the 1940s Truman boldly presented a major reorientation of American foreign policy to a Republican Congress in the hope that bipartisan consent could be mobilized within, or close to, his deadline. His hope was realized. Other explanations of the tractability of public opinion in the 1940s point to a new turn in the cycle of mood from isolationism to internationalism. The problem with this explanation is that until the Truman Doctrine was proclaimed, internationalism was understood to mean "making collective security work." It was a major goal of Truman and his advisers to substitute for this form of internationalism recognition and acceptance of America's own responsibilities for maintaining world order.

This study does not deny the importance of any of these explanations for the activism of the 1940s in contrast to the isolationism of the 1930s. Rather it directs attention to another set of changes that altered policy makers' sense of the possible. These changes occurred within the linkages between domestic opinion and the decision-making process. In 1937 Roosevelt lacked many of the amenities for relating his foreign policies to the condition of public opinion that were available to Truman ten years later. Without systematic analysis and submission of public-opinion data, it was easy to assume that the isolationism of the mass public was as resolute as that of the Congress. Evidence presented later in this chapter suggests that this assumption was only partially justified. Relying mainly on congressional opinion, White House mail, and conversations with political intimates Roosevelt construed public opinion in ways that conformed with his predilection for caution. Even the part of the press reaction to his quarantine proposal that was sympathetic was filtered out of the policy process. Initially favorable reactions faded away when the administration declined to lobby for a major reorientation in the policy of isolation and neutrality. Fireside chats were not followed up by a sustained public-information program.

Although the administration had no scruples about mounting "educational" capaigns aimed at mobilizing the public behind New Deal social security legislation, Roosevelt did not consider raising a similar challenge to Congress over neutrality. The president accepted the prerogatives Congress had asserted in removing this "crucial area of foreign relations from executive control."[1] His deference to Congress persisted until Pearl Harbor. Only with the outbreak of war did the president claim the same prerogatives in mobilizing the public behind his foreign policy that he enjoyed in domestic policy.

Contrast this situation with the one facing Truman in 1947. The war had legitimized a far more active role for the executive in foreign affairs and had revolutionized the opinion-policy relationship. By institutionalizing procedures for the analysis and transmission of public opinion data to policy makers, it created the precedents and machinery for domestic information campaigns on foreign-policy issues. Armed with accurate public-opinion reports, policy makers could identify potential sources of opposition and support. Policies could be formulated and presented in ways designed to neutralize opposition and accentuate support. Armed with a "public affairs" educational facility, the State Department could rapidly mount a campaign to mobilize consent for new foreign-policy initiatives. This it did successfully twice in three years: first, in 1944 and 1945, to boost the Dumbarton Oaks proposals and the San Francisco conference founding the United Nations; and, second, in 1947, to win popular approval for aid to Greece and Turkey. To be sure, much had changed between 1937 and 1947 in addition to the government's machinery for managing public opinion. But any account of the impact of public opinion on foreign policy would be deficient if it did not take this particular linkage into account.

This chapter challenges the once traditional interpretation of Roosevelt's retreat from the quarantine proposal as a classic example of the public-opinion constraint. It argues that the constraint emanated not from the mass public or even from the press but from a projection of congressional isolation on to the country at large. Roosevelt's intuitive analysis of public reaction to his Chicago speech encouraged him to believe that popular isolationism obliged Congress to reject any but the most nebulous cautionary gestures toward the Axis. A systematic analysis of public opinion reveals a more permissive opinion environment, which would probably have been amenable to strong leadership.

Once external events persuaded Roosevelt and his advisers to challenge the most egregious portions of isolationist legislation—initially the arms embargo—the government seized the role of opinion maker. Success in this role owed much to the deterioration of the international situation and the cumulative effect on public opinion of Japanese and German depredations. But public-opinion data do not support the view that shifts in policy occurred only as "graduated responses" to shifts in public opinion. There was a two-way flow of opinion; public opinion both responded to and stimulated increasingly bold measures of assistance to the Allies.

In brief, this was not a classic example of the public-opinion constraint, if by that term one implies a prohibition on certain policy options imposed by the public at large. Rather, lacking confidence in their role as opinion makers, Roosevelt and his advisers ignored positive signals from the public and bowed to congressional isolationism. The assumption that this isolationism amounted to the views of the mass public, writ large, was never seriously questioned. Historians are far from agreed about Roosevelt's own policy preferences at the time. But a politician's sense of the desirable cannot be divorced from his sense of the possible; and this, it will be argued, was influenced by the condition of the opinion-policy relationship. In making this argument we shall focus on the quarantine speech, because it is so often written of as an example of the public-opinion constraint, and on the repeal of the arms embargo, because here, for the first time, the government and its articulate supporters grasped their potential power as opinion makers.

APPEASEMENT AS A REFLECTION OF PUBLIC OPINION

"During the years between 1935 and 1937," Thomas Bailey wrote, "a peace-obsessed public opinion foisted upon the administration 'permanent' neutrality legislation, as though one could legislate permanence in a world of change."[2] Despite spectacular acts of foreign aggression, Bailey argued, the secretary of state and president could not step beyond the limits of isolation and neutrality without jeopardizing their claim to the country's allegiance. But the isolationism, to which Bailey attributes such compelling power, was not an homogeneous phenomenon. There were conservative and radical varieties;[3] isolationism sprang from hatred of war,[4] from pacifism, from dislike of arms profiteering, from fears of renewed depression, from sympathies with communism or fascism or from disdain toward both. Some isolationists were pro-German, others were patriotic, Anglophobes. Agreement did not go beyond the conviction that America ought to preserve its freedom of action in world affairs, at almost any price.

The Nazis took considerable comfort from the prevalence of isolationism in America. In 1937 the German Foreign Office was receiving reports that foreshadow Professor Bailey's analysis of the public-opinion constraint. American foreign policy, the German ambassador reported, would tilt toward the democracies only when public opinion grasped the true consequences of American neutrality.[5] The State Department made a similar analysis in its review of American foreign policy in the decade between 1931 and 1941. Published in 1943, this document was the first full-scale official attempt to attribute the persistence of isolationism and appeasement to American public opinion:

During a large part of the period with which this volume deals [1931-1941], much of public opinion in this country did not accept the thesis that a European war could vitally affect the security of the United States or that an attack on the United States by any of the Axis powers was possible. In this respect it differed from the President and the Secretary of State who early became convinced that the aggressive policies of the Axis powers were directed toward an ultimate attack on the United States and that, therefore, our foreign relations should be so conducted as to give all possible support to the nations endeavoring to check the march of Axis aggression.

Our foreign policy during the decade under consideration necessarily had to move within the framework of a gradual evolution of public opinion in the United States away from the idea of isolation expressed in "neutrality" legislation and toward realization that the Axis design was a plan of world conquest in which the United States was intended to be a certain, though perhaps ultimate, victim and that our prime policy, therefore, must be defense against actual and mounting danger. This was an important factor influencing the conduct of our foreign relations. [6]

Two basic points can be distilled from these paragraphs: first, public opinion had become wedded to isolationism and, second, the president and secretary of state disagreed with but were constrained by the popular mood. [7]

The State Department analysis, like that of Lloyd Free and other scholars, [8] postulates a kind of graduated response by the government to shifts in public opinion. In 1936 popular pacifism resounded in the president's speech at Chautauqua. In 1937 at Chicago, the president's proposal to quarantine the aggressors did not echo public sentiment and so was hastily withdrawn. Each subsequent step toward greater American involvement in the world crises *followed* a new step in the public's harsh schooling in international events. Critical decisions included repeal of the arms embargo provision of the Neutrality Act, the agreement to exchange refitted destroyers for British bases, lend-lease, and the convoying of merchant ships across the Atlantic. Each of these steps, according to the "graduated-response" theory, only became possible once public opinion had been jolted by the fear that the latest excesses of the Axis threatened the Western Hemisphere.

Roosevelt's October 1937 Chicago speech is generally taken as the first clear sign that his administration had become dissatisfied with the strategy of isolation. The speech is usually interpreted as a "trial balloon," which was instantly deflated when the public responded negatively. This deflation is considered evidence of the operation of a powerful public-opinion constraint.

But this interpretation has not stood up to critical scrutiny. It rests on an "historical legend," according to Dorothy Borg.[9] The trial balloon (or opinion constraint) version of Roosevelt's retreat from the quarantine speech fails on two counts: first, the administration had not decided on, and so could not have been testing, any definite course of action; and second, the public response was not overwhelmingly negative.[10]

On the first point, Borg's analysis of the drafting of the speech revealed that it had not been intended as the clarion call to resist Japanese aggression of subsequent mythology. When the president went to Chicago he had no specific plan in mind but rather hoped to stimulate discussion of *some* scheme to ensure an enduring peace. Because the League of Nations condemned Japan the very next day, observers tended to link the president's speech with a wider policy of sanctions. None, however, had been intended. Roosevelt was groping for some "means of getting the dictatorships and democracies to make a concerted effort to ensure peace."[11] Until then he had had little success; Neville Chamberlain, the British Prime Minister, reacted badly to the president's proposals, preferring his own search for political appeasement to grandiose American schemes based on disarmament and international law.

If the mechanical opinion constraint model fails in light of the president's intentions, it also fails in light of the public response. Although the speech offered no more than verbal gestures toward the avoidance of war, these gestures elicited a far more positive response than has generally been thought. Gallup polls had not yet been established as required presidential reading, but surveys of press reaction, a source of public opinion the President closely followed, indicated a mixed reaction, by no means overwhelmingly negative. Approval was also reflected in the White House mail.

The *New York Times* found "general approval of the President's address in Chicago calling upon peace-loving peoples to make a concerted effort in opposition to aggressor nations which are creating lawlessness in the world."[12] For all the vagueness of Roosevelt's proposal to "quarantine" aggressor nations, many leader writers believed that it marked a welcome and decisive break from the policy of isolation. The *Pioneer Press* of St. Paul, Minnesota, called the Chicago address "the most significant speech he [the president] has made on American foreign policy because it aligns him definitely with the Woodrow Wilson viewpoint of world co-operation rather than the isolationist policies which have prevailed since the war." [13]

The *Cincinnati Enquirer* was "gratified" that "President Roosevelt at last has spoken in this vein, offering at least a hint that he will adopt a stronger foreign policy—one designed to give real assistance to the peaceful nations already straining to repress international gangsterism." [14] Even the Republican *Philadelphia Inquirer* believed that "every right-thinking American citizen will heartily endorse President Roosevelt's burning denunciation of the terrorism and international lawlessness which today are disgracing our world civilization." [15] Pointedly, the *Inquirer* also praised the speech for its resolution "to keep this country out of war." The paper hinted that the former objective and the latter might not prove entirely compatible; pitfalls were to be expected on the road to peace.

Critical reaction fastened as much on the vagueness of Roosevelt's proposals as on the likelihood of their leading to war. The *New York Herald Tribune* mentioned that the Council of the League of Nations had made many people indignant by "its extremely cautious approach to an anti-Japanese resolution." But, despite the League's vacillations, it at least had definite verbal sanctions in mind.

> President Roosevelt, for all his eloquence at Chicago, cannot be credited with anything so specific. His world audience no doubt thinks that much of his speech had reference to Japan. But he did not say so. His talk of "quarantine" may be construed as an endorsement of economic sanctions, but he did not mention them. His appeal was wholly emotional. It named no names, it cited no specific treaty clauses that are in default and no specific way of resenting treaty violation. If it was an appeal for anything it was for a popular emotional mandate to the President to take whatever course in our international relations seemed to him best. [16]

Commenting on foreign reaction, other editorial writers took up the charge that the speech could mean all things to all men. "In Berlin," the *Des Moines Register* observed:

The official spokesman airily assumed that the President's reference was to Japan. In Rome well-informed sources said that the President's reference was to Russia. "Italy," said one of the officials "is a peace-loving nation." [17]

In his column in the New York Times Arthur Krock also pointed out that the people of the world could probably not even hazard a "good guess" at the target of Roosevelt's remarks. The dictators could bend the speech to their own purposes. Krock learned the day after the speech that "in Berlin yesterday there was at least a pretended disposition to believe that the shoe flung by the President fits Russia perfectly and not Germany at all."

These criticisms sprang from the suspicion that the president, far from advocating a policy that would lead the country to war, still had no policy at all. News dispatches freely speculated that the announcement of a boycott against Japan was imminent. But Krock's enquiries at the State Department unearthed only official perplexity: "The fact is that the department is not advised of any specific plan he has in mind whereby the United States, with other great democratic powers, will attempt to compel the dictators to 'desist' from invasion of alien territory and participation in foreign civil wars." [18]

It is clear that much press reaction was supportive of the president's speech, believing it to be a needed departure from the "ostrich hunt for security" (Washington Post) embodied in the Neutrality Act. Independent, Democratic, and Republican organs of opinion urged the translation of the president's emotional words into a concrete action program.

Approval was not, of course, unanimous. As Borg notes, "There was a barrage from prominent isolationists" and from the Hearst press. Not all Republican journals confined themselves to mild warnings about possible pitfalls on the road to peace. The Boston Herald delivered a severe warning: "It may be true that 'the very foundations of civilization are seriously threatened.' But this time, Mr. President, Americans will not be stampeded into going 3,000 miles across water to save them. Crusade if you must, but for the sake of several millions of American mothers confine your expanding to the continental limits of America." [19]

Hearst intervened personally in mounting a congressional and press campaign against the notion of a quarantine. This action probably affected Roosevelt deeply. At one other apparent turning point in his career—during his campaign for the Democratic nomination in 1932—

Roosevelt had ridden to success only after acceding to Hearst's demand that he repudiate the League of Nations and with it his link to Wilsonian internationalism. "Few men were better acquainted with the range of Mr. Hearst's power than Governor Roosevelt and his immediate associates," Charles Beard has written.[20] Hearst applied considerable pressure to obtain Roosevelt's recantation in 1932. When the governor offered his assurances in private the press baron insisted that they be made public lest he be thought to be "hiding his opinions from the public and only expressing them privately to people whose support he wants."[21]

With memories such as these it is, perhaps, not surprising that Roosevelt felt particularly susceptible to taunts from the Hearst press, even from the eminence of five years as President. He expressed his annoyance to several close associates and, at the press conference the day after the Chicago speech, singled out "the old man of the seas—old man Hearst" for a "perfectly terrible—awful" editorial interpreting the speech as a call to arms.[22]

Despite evidence that Roosevelt was aware of the favorable elements in the public response,[23] negative comment was far more salient to him. Cordell Hull added a conception of the general public as a potentially hostile, isolationist monolith when stirred by the prospect of war.[24] With important segments of opinion mobilized against the administration's domestic policies, it seemed vital not to arouse the isolationists in Congress to new levels of fear and distrust.

By October 12 something of a retreat from the limited promise of Chicago was underway. In a fireside chat the president rather cryptically drew his listeners' attention to the lessons he had drawn from his years in the Navy Department: "Remember that from 1913 to 1921 I personally was fairly close to world events and in that period while I learned much of what to do I also learned what not to do."[25] Since these words admitted two possible interpretations, the president came down heavily on the negative by repeating the formula: "America hates war." Nothing as definite as sanctions had been intended at Chicago but many people assumed that this was the implication. Fears were circulating that Roosevelt would endorse League of Nations sanctions and that sanctions meant war. The president sought to remove this impression by uttering reassuringly pacific generalities.

This partial retreat, as well as America's general posture of detachment, has often been laid at the door of public opinion. This was the "official version" of the persistence of isolation propounded by the State

Department in its documentary collection *Peace and War*. And Roosevelt undoubtedly perceived the attitudes of the mass public as a factor that limited America's freedom to maneuver. According to Sumner Welles, "The President had determined to make a vigorous effort to persuade public opinion that in its own interests the United States should propose some constructive plan for international action to check the forces of aggression before they succeeded in engulfing the world." [26] Undoubtedly Welles, like the official version, indulges in post-facto wisdom. Yet Roosevelt's sensitivity to public opinion was genuine; it was not simply a ploy to avoid diplomatic entanglements. [27]

But did the president's perceptions correspond with the findings of the polls? How strong was public opposition to American entanglement in the affairs of the world? It is important to ask these questions. The argument of Bailey, the State Department, and others that a "peace-obsessed public" "foisted" upon Roosevelt the policy of nonintervention depends on the intractability of isolationist sentiment among the general public.

In a memorandum for Norman Davis, America's ambassador to the Nine Power Conference in Brussels, Roosevelt expressed concern lest American freedom of action should appear to be jeopardized by too intimate relations with the League. [28] Did this fear reflect the disposition of popular opinion? A poll taken in October 1937, the month of the quarantine speech, indicates that most Americans with opinions on the subject continued to oppose American membership in the League. To the question "Would you like to see the United States join the League of Nations?" 26 percent responded positively, 52 percent responded negatively, and 22 percent held no opinion. [29] A breakdown of these figures by presidential preference in table 1 suggests that those who had voted for Roosevelt were somewhat better disposed toward American membership than were those who had voted for Landon in 1936.

TABLE 1
Would You Like to See the United States Join the League of Nations?

	Yes	No	No Opinion
Total	26%	52%	22%
Roosevelt voters	27	50	23
Landon voters	19	63	18

Source: AIPO Poll, October 18, 1937.

Only half of Roosevelt's electoral constituency opposed American membership in the League while slightly more than a quarter favored it. On the other hand close to two-thirds of those who had voted for the Republican presidential candidate opposed American membership in the League. This poll appeared twelve days after the quarantine speech, but it is impossible to know whether the interviews were conducted in time to measure the impact of the speech. Furthermore we do not have trend data for the purposes of comparison.

Did opposition to League membership spring from an isolationist reflex or from a considered judgment of its effectiveness? The October 1937 poll provides no means of distinguishing underlying sentiments, but earlier polls suggest an answer. In 1936 *Fortune* asked, "If war in Europe is averted through the League of Nations, do you believe the United States should join the League?" The response was "yes," 30 percent; "no," 57 percent; "no opinion," 13 percent.[30] Problems of comparability, particularly acute in these early polls, prevent any but the most schematic inferences from these results. At the very least we can see that even the hypothetical success of the League, posited in January 1936, did not arouse public enthusiasm for membership. By 1937 the replacement of the hypothetical success of the League in the above question by its manifest failure to curb Axis aggression in the Rhineland, Spain, Ethiopia, and China had little noticeable impact on the public's attitude.

When asked directly about the contribution of the League to the prospects of peace, the public divided in a similar manner. In December 1937 28 percent of Gallup's respondents felt that the cause of world peace would be hurt if the League of Nations were dissolved, 48 percent felt that this would not hurt peace prospects, and 24 percent held no opinion.[31] Considering the late date of the poll, its result may, perhaps, be attributed both to the manifest failures of the League and to visceral isolationism.

The general profile emerging from these polls is one of an isolationist but divided public whose attitude toward the League probably had little to do with its merits as a peace-keeping organization. The fact that almost half of the respondents either favored League entry or had no opinion somewhat mitigates the picture of a resolutely isolationist public. The fluctuation of "don't knows" around the 20 percent to 25 percent level suggests that a pool of potential recruits to the principle of collective security existed. The upward trend between 1941 and 1945 in those believing that the United States should have joined the League in 1919 supports this view.[32]

The most that can be inferred from these polls is that antileague views predominated among, but did not monopolize, the opinion-holding sectors of the public. As for the articulate strata, we have seen that opinion was divided. Over the nebulous proposal to "quarantine the aggressors"—a plan most readily translated into closer cooperation with the League policy of sanctions—opinion was negative but not overwhelmingly so. There was considerable evidence of approval as well as disapproval of Roosevelt's Chicago speech, which came to the attention of the administration.

The disposition of public opinion can scarcely be said to have intervened to prevent the implementation of policies upon which the administration had decided. But to an administration whose hesitancy was bolstered by the tangible weight of congressional isolationism, mass opinion appeared as an added constraint. A predisposition toward caution coupled with the threat of congressional censure can filter a policy maker's perceptions of the views of the wider public. As a man of extreme political wariness, already confronting serious opposition to his domestic policies, Roosevelt was, no doubt, especially sensitized to negative signals from the public.

At Chautauqua in 1936, the president had referred to the need to encourage a body of public opinion committed to the maintenance of peace.[33] But after this speech the drift in government policy suggested either that no opinion-building channels were available or that Roosevelt was unwilling to use them. In 1937 Roosevelt had not yet begun to receive Hadley Cantril's analyses of public opinion. No procedures had been established for the regular transmission of the findings of even the new commercial polls to the president, so he could be more easily swayed by a subjective interpretation of the popular mood, based on congressional opinion, the mail, and the counsel of close advisers. Cordell Hull's influence was largely restricted to foreign economic policy and here, at least, a limited capability had been established for the mobilization of support for the reciprocal trade agreements.[34] But outside of this narrow sphere there was neither machinery nor precedent for efforts to "lobby" opinion on behalf of a reorientation in the country's foreign policy. The story of the arms embargo repeal in 1939, and more generally of the emergency agencies established between 1939 and 1941, suggests that as soon as events pushed the government to the point of decision, channels were rapidly created for the mobilization of consent.

REPEAL OF THE ARMS EMBARGO

The first decisive step toward abandoning isolationism came in November 1939 when Congress finally repealed the arms embargo provision of the Neutrality Act, which had stood since 1935. Neutrality had not operated impartially in the undeclared war in China and the Spanish civil war. In both cases the embargo had far more serious consequences for the parties resisting Axis aggression. The embargo also undermined the desperate attempt of France and Britain to avoid war with Germany. The British and French prime ministers, Chamberlain and Daladier, pressed the United States for repeal, but the embargo stood through Munich, the Anchluss, the Crystal Night, and even the occupation of Czechoslovakia. Only the invasion of Poland and the coming of war to Britain and France persuaded the administration to mobilize the public for repeal.

In this section we shall examine public attitudes on issues that pertain to the arms embargo and, more generally, to isolationism. We shall also discuss the semiofficial informational activities that helped secure repeal in 1939. These activities were the prototypes for unofficial internationalist agitation during World War II and influenced the government's own public information strategy in support of the U.N. charter in 1944 and 1945. [35]

The viability of isolationism depends on the perceived capacity of the nation to remain insulated from foreign conflicts. [36] Its morality, if one is needed, depends on the absence of relevant ethical distinctions between the parties to such conflicts. Once either of these conditions is undermined the doctrine begins to appear as a euphemism for defeatism or appeasement.

INSULATION

Between 1937 and 1939 the American Institute for Public Opinion (AIPO) asked several questions designed to elicit the public's view of the credibility of American insulation. The series indicated in table 2 provides a general indication of the trend, although allowance must be made for differences in question wording, sample size, and sampling technique. For our purposes the overall magnitudes rather than the precise figures are sufficient. Unfortunately Gallup often discarded data on the percentage of voters having no opinion. Where available this figure is given. In all cases, however, positive and negative responses are given as percentages of the responses of only those subjects who held an opinion.

TABLE 2
Will America Be Drawn into a European War?

		Yes	No	No Opinion
April	1936 [a]	44%	56%	
July	1938 [b]	46	54	
September	1938 [c]	68	32	11%
April	1939 [d]	58	42	
August	1939 [e]	60	40	14
September	1939 [f]	76	24	

[a] AIPO April 4, 1936: "Do you think the United States will be drawn into the next European war?

[b] Ibid., July 27, 1938: "If England and France have a war with Germany and Italy, do you think the United States can stay out?" A comparable section was asked: "If England and France have a war with Germany and Italy, do you think the United States will stay out?" Results were combined. In table 2, the "yes" column indicates those respondents who believed that the United States would be drawn into a European war, regardless of whether Gallup phrased the question in terms of being drawn in or being able to keep out.

[c] Ibid., September 23, 1938: "If England and France have a war against Germany and Italy, do you think the United States will be drawn into it?"

[d] Ibid., April 16, 1939: "If there is a [European] war [this year] do you think the United States will be drawn into it?"

[e] Ibid., August 30, 1939: "Do you think the United States will be drawn into this war?"
[f] Ibid., September 3, 1939: "If England and France have a war against Germany and Italy, do you think the United States will be drawn in?"

Despite problems of comparability the orders of magnitude in these marginals are sufficiently consistent to permit some general conclusions. In the early period a small plurality of those with opinions believed that American insulation from a new European war was feasible. As the situation deteriorated a majority reached the conclusion that America would inevitably be drawn in. This realistic judgment coexisted with a continued preference for noninvolvement. As late as April 1939, 95 percent of

Gallup respondents with opinions opposed an American declaration of war in the event that Germany, Italy, France, and Britain became belligerents. [37] In February 1939 66 percent of all Gallup respondents felt that the United States should help neither side in such a conflict.[38] In April 1939 65 percent still opposed aid to Britain and France if this threatened to bring about American involvement, a figure that remained fairly steady even after the outbreak of hostilities. In August and again in October majorities opposed American troop involvement in Europe even if it appeared that Britain and France faced defeat.

ETHICAL DISTINCTIONS BETWEEN THE AXIS AND THE ALLIES?

One of the isolationist themes that appealed to the spirit of American independence was the ubiquity of corruption on the old continent. Not until 1942, when America had been drawn into the war as an ally of the Soviet Union, could a majority of respondents to the Fortune poll choose between communism and fascism. Father Coughlin, the Detroit radio priest, and other Anglophobe or pro-German isolationists sought to instill a similar indifference between British and German "imperialism." It was against this image of the moral equivalence of the Axis and its enemies that groups like the Non-Partisan Committee for Peace through Revision of the Neutrality Law directed publicity. William Allen White attacked this issue directly in a speech he gave on behalf of the committee on October 15, 1939. The European struggle, White said,

is not a contest of imperialist nations struggling for place and power. It is a clash of ideologies. In Germany and in Russia, the state is master of the citizen. In the democracies of Europe—France and England, Holland and the Scandinavian countries, the citizens control the state. The struggle of two thousand years for human liberty has been wiped out east of the Rhine. . . . These European democracies are carrying our banner, fighting the American battle. [39]

This speech was recorded and widely distributed for replaying by phonograph. When the picture of America's own entanglement in war was removed, the public appeared readier to express a preference between the Axis and the Allies and to offer all aid short of war. Of course it is hard to assess the relative impact of world events themselves and the publicity given to them by speeches like the one quoted above. On the one hand the public could be expected to empathize with Britain's predicament far more than with that of, say, Spain. There were stronger cultural affinities, and the issue was not confused by the clash of communism, fascism, and even anarchism. But on the other hand, the "phoney war" was no more spectacular than the many demarches of Japan, Italy, and Germany during the 1930s, and empathy with Britain was mixed with large doses of Anglophobia, particularly among German-, Italian-, and Irish-Americans.

Whatever the determinants of public attitudes the poll shown in table 3, taken the same month as White's speech, indicates the development of

TABLE 3
Do You Favor Repeal of the Arms Embargo?

	Yes	No	No Opinion
Favor repeal of arms embargo if this helps Germany	4%	91%	5%
Favor repeal of arms embargo if this helps Britain and France?	58	34	8

Source: AIPO, October 18, 1939: "If the repeal of the arms embargo would help Germany, but not England and France, would you favor such a repeal?" "If the repeal of the arms embargo would help England and France but not Germany would you favor such repeal?"

partisanship. Clearly the public's willingness to abandon the arms embargo had become dependent on the likely impact of such a move on the war in Europe. In Asia too the public's incipient partisanship became more marked with every Japanese military success. Public sympathies had been with China ever since the first Japanese assults on the mainland. But for many years the struggle in the Far East had been of low salience to the public. As Japanese imperialism blended in the public mind with Axis aggression in Europe, sympathies with China rose and the proportion of the public with no opinion fell (table 4). By 1940 the percentage of respondents unable to choose between China and Japan had fallen from a high of 55 percent to 22 percent while a full three-quarters of the sample expressed their sympathy with China. By November 1939, when the arms embargo was repealed, only small segments of the public continued to view the world crisis as a clash of rival imperialisms equally undeserving of American sympathy and support.

TABLE 4
Which Side Do You Prefer: China or Japan?

	China	Japan	Neither
August 1937	43%	2%	55%
October 1937	59	1	40
May 1939	73	2	25
February 1940	76	2	22

Source: AIPO, August 2, 1937: "Which side [are your sympathies on in the present fight between Japan and China]?" October 4, 1937: "In the present fight between China and Japan, are your sympathies with China, Japan, or neither side?" May 19, 1939: "In the present war between Japan and China, which side do you sympathize with?" February 20, 1940: "In the present war between Japan and China which side do you want to see win?"

Although public confidence in the viability of American insulation was on the decline and public sympathies with the victims of Axis aggression were on the rise, large segments clung to the belief that direct American involvement should be avoided. In September 1939 the prognosis of 76 percent of Gallup respondents with opinions was that the United States would be drawn into the war in Europe; but virtually no one was prepared to translate that prognosis into the prescription that the United States *ought* to declare war and send its troops to the defense of the democracies. Once war had actually materialized sentiment in favor of nonintervention became almost unanimous, as table 5 shows. There was also a wishful reversion to the belief that America need not necessarily be drawn in, with 60 percent of those with opinions taking this position in a late September poll. [40]

By November 1939 the prescription chosen by the largest group of respondents to a Fortune poll corresponded closely with that which the president sought in repealing the arms embargo: "Take no sides and offer to sell anything to anybody, but make them pay cash and take it away in their own ships." [41] This prescription represented the public victory of the cash-and-carry compromise first suggested by Bernard Baruch in 1937. It summed up the ambivalence of the public between growing partisan sympathies and a persistent "illusion of neutrality."

TABLE 5
Should America Send Its Forces to Europe to Fight Germany?

		Yes	No	Don't Know
March	1939	17%	83%	
May	1939	16	84	
August	1939	8	90	2%
September	1939	6	94	

Source: AIPO, March 12, 1939: "In case such a war [German and Italy versus England and France] breaks out, how far should we go in helping England and France—should we send our army and navy abroad to fight the enemies of England and France?" Alternative wording, results combined: ". . . to help England and France?" May 3, 1939: "In case Germany and Italy go to war against England and France, how far should we go in helping England and France? Should we send our army and navy abroad to fight Germany and France?" August 30, 1939: "Do you think the United States should declare war on Germany at once and send our army and navy abroad to help England, France and Poland?" September 11, 1939: "What should be the policy of the United States in the present European war—should we declare war and send our army and navy abroad to fight Germany"?

These poll findings suggest the following:

1. That by 1939 the public had abandoned one of the canons of isolationism: failure to perceive relevant ethical distinctions between the parties to foreign wars.
2. That the credibility of American insularity fell between 1936 and 1939.
3. But that even while insularity looked less viable the public clung to hopes of noninvolvement.

Taken together, public attitudes on these and other issues pertaining to isolationism were ambivalent. Attitudes with conflicting implications for American policy coexisted. On the one hand there were profound sympathies for China and the democracies and an impulse to assist them, as long as this would not bring war to America. On the other hand there was widespread attachment to the amoral policy of neutrality. Repeal of the arms embargo came to be preferred to an avowed American policy of aid to the Allies.

The graduated-response interpretation of the opinion-policy relationship considers shifts in policy to be possible only when preceded by shifts in relevant public attitudes. But this interpretation fails to take into account the fact that public attitudes are often ambivalent, containing divergent policy implications. This ambivalence, reinforced by the low salience of even critical foreign-policy issues, can create a permissive opinion climate in which a resolute decision maker can mobilize support for policy innovations. This is exactly what happened in 1939 when public opinion was divided on the major issues of peace and war. International events in Europe and the Far East had injected a stream of realism into the public's conception of American insularity, but they had not produced widespread sentiment in favor of intervention. On the contrary, significant strands of isolationism persisted. As soon as the president resolved to lift the arms embargo he established links with extragovernmental opinion groups sharing the same objective. A concerted information campaign was mounted unofficially with the president's concurrence and support. Taken together, the deterioration of the international situation and the campaign for repeal induced the Congress to do away with the arms embargo that had stood for four years.

The Non-Partisan Committee for Peace through Revision of the Neutrality Law was the organization that spearheaded the campaign for repeal.[42] The committee, and its Republican chairman William Allen White, editor of the *Emporia* (Kansas) *Gazette*, attacked isolationist opposition to repeal. They strove to undermine isolationist insistence on the equally undeserving nature of German and British "imperialism." White enlisted the support of professional, religious, academic, and political leaders, including newspaper publishers. The *Chicago Daily News*, published by Colonel Frank Knox in the heart of the isolationist belt, was particularly forthcoming in support of the campaign.

The Committee to Defend America by Aiding the Allies succeeded the first White committee in mobilizing support for the destroyers-for-bases deal with Britain, lend-lease, and the decision to patrol the north Atlantic. Both committees acknowledged that they were involved in a "purely propaganda job" and for this and other reasons maintained their independence of the administration. Such independence was vital in 1940, an election year, when key committee members, including White, threw their support to Wendell Willkie, the Republican presidential candidate. Since Willkie shared most of the president's views on the world crisis, this did not impede the campaign.

Despite its independence, the committee enjoyed close links with Roosevelt. As White said of his relations with the president: "I knew I had his private support. . . . I never did anything the President didn't ask for, and I always conferred with him on our program." [43] White repeatedly urged the president to seize the initiative in order to mobilize consent for the policy they both preferred. On a very bleak day in 1940, June 5, when the defeat of France was almost complete, White told the president by telegram: "You will not be able to lead the American people unless you catch up with them. They are going fast." [44]

This chapter's analysis of a "classic example" of the public-opinion constraint suggests:

1. That Roosevelt had no definite proposal in mind when he made his quarantine speech in Chicago.
2. That public reaction to the speech was mixed. It included approval and indifference as well as disapproval of a more active stand against the Nazis.
3. That, being divided, public opinion was more permissive and hence more susceptible than Roosevelt believed to a strong presidential lead between 1937 and 1939.
4. That lacking the facilities for a systematic study of public opinion, Roosevelt was able to project his own hesitancy on to the mass public, magnifying congressional opposition into a solid wall of public isolationism. This deferred action even when popular isolationism was crumbling.
5. And that once the president, aided by the White committee decided to mobilize support for a firmer stand by challenging the arms embargo, Congress and the general public fell into line.

With little systematization of the linkages between the mass public and policy makers, the latter are forced to rely on "intuitive" measures of popular sentiment. Without a direct line to vox populi there is little alternative to the legislature's claim to embody the wishes of the American people. If legislative opinion is concerted and threatening, the president can, like Roosevelt, exaggerate to himself the recalcitrance of popular opinion. This reduces his sense of the possible and builds mass opinion, with all its divergent tendencies, into a hostile monolith.

The repeal of the arms embargo gave Roosevelt his first experience of what it meant to be an *opinion maker* in foreign affairs. Subsequently his advisers urged him to realize the full potential of his office for opinion leadership. During the course of the war the president became more inclined to accept this advice. National emergency thrust upon him unusual prerogatives and put at his disposal what his congressional foes considered to be a domestic propaganda agency. This revolutionized the relationship between foreign policy and public opinion.

NOTES

1. Arthur M. Schlesinger, Jr., *The Imperial Republic* (New York, 1973), p. 98; Elmer E. Cornwell, *Presidential Leadership of Public Opinion* (Bloomington, 1964), p. 141.
2. Thomas A. Bailey, *The Man in the Street* (New York, 1948), p. 8.
3. For a discussion of the varieties of isolationism, see Manfred Jonas, *Isolationism in America, 1935-1941* (New York, 1966), pp. 32-69.
4. Jerome S. Bruner includes "hatred of war" among the six cardinal convictions of the American people with respect to foreign policy. The other five are: the sense of geographical isolation, faith in the nation's security, the feeling of political stability, the humane point of view, and suspicion of foreign powers. Hatred of war in the 1930s sprang from memories of World War I and disappointed hopes in the League of Nations. "No nation can exist," Bruner wrote in 1944, "which regards the absence of war as more important than any other national value. Hitler's expansion in Europe and Japan's in the Far East would never have reached their bloated proportions had that fact been realized in the Allied world sooner." Bruner, *Mandate from the People* (New York, 1944), pp. 10-18. As early as 1944 scholars were drawing conclusions from the appeasement experience that affected their perception of the requisites for peace in the postwar world.
5. Jonas, *Isolationism in America*, p. 208.
6. Department of State, *Peace and War: United States Foreign Policy, 1931-1941* (Washington, D.C., 1943), cited by Charles A. Beard, *American Foreign Policy in the Making, 1932-1940* (New Haven, 1946), p. 29, and by Walter Johnson, *The Battle Against Isolation* (Chicago, 1944), p. 12.
7. Beard subjects these paragraphs to the tests of "etymology, philology and grammar" and finds them lacking. "The country" is so abstract that it ignores the whole question of the stratification of public opinion, which was discussed in chapter 1. The word "early" leaves open the question of when, during an entire decade, policy makers decided that the Axis must be resisted. And, finally, the view that the president must "move within the framework" of an evolving public opinion leaves open the question of his degree of freedom. See Beard, *American Foreign Policy*, pp. 29-35.
8. See Lloyd A. Free, "The Introversion-Extroversion Cycle in National Mood during Recent Decades" (paper prepared for delivery at the Annual Conference of the American Association for Public Opinion Research, May 18, 1973).
9. Dorothy Borg, "Notes on Roosevelt's 'Quarantine' Speech," *Political Science Quarterly*, 72 (1957).

10. For a recent endorsement of Borg's thesis, see Bernard C. Cohen, *The Public's Impact on Foreign Policy* (Boston, 1973), p. 71.
11. Borg, "Notes."
12. *New York Times*, October 6, 1937.
13. *Pioneer Press* (St. Paul), October 6, 1937.
14. *Cincinnati Enquirer*, October 6, 1937.
15. *Philadelphia Inquirer*, October 6, 1937.
16. *New York Herald Tribune*. October 6, 1937.
17. *Des Moines Register*, October 6, 1937.
18. *New York Times*, October 6, 1937. Krock concludes that rather than seeking any particular policy at Chicago, Roosevelt was "but mobilizing and articulating the public opinion of one of the most powerful of the nations in the hope that somehow his words would burst the barrier of censorship erected by the dictators."
19. *Boston Herald*, October 6, 1937.
20. Beard, *American Foreign Policy*, pp. 72-73.
21. Hearst to E. D. Coblentz, January 21, 1932, cited by ibid., p. 74.
22. Press conference transcript, cited by Borg, "Notes," p. 432.
23. Cohen, *The Public's Impact*, p. 71.
24. On Hull's sensitivity to isolationist opinion, see Donald Watt, "Roosevelt and Chamberlain, Two Appeasers," *International Journal* (Spring 1973).
25. *New York Times*, October 13, 1937.
26. To Welles the quarantine speech was a first tentative step in this direction. Borg compares this analysis, made by Welles in 1944, with a later one in which he reverted to the view that Roosevelt had in mind an actual embargo against Japan when he gave the Chicago speech. Borg, "Notes," p. 418.
27. Besides Roosevelt's personal sensitivities he depended on the support of several notable isolationists for the passage of his domestic legislation. His hesitancy, therefore, can be explained both by exaggerated perceptions of hostility to his proposal from the wider public and by sound political prudence vis à vis Congress.
28. Memorandum from the file of President Roosevelt's Secretary, *Foreign Relations of the United States* (Washington, D.C., 1937), p. 85. The memorandum gave Davis instructions for the forthcoming conference. He was to make it clear that "the United States cannot afford to be made in public opinion at home a tail to the British kite, as has been charged, and is now being charged by the Hearst press and others." He was to press for modest, joint approaches to the problem of peace and not take a more forthright stand than, it was believed, American public opinion would tolerate.
29. AIPO Poll, October 18, 1937. Hadley Cantril and Mildred Strunk, eds., *Public Opinion, 1935-1946* (Princeton, 1951), p. 403. Wherever possible the AIPO marginals have been transformed to show the number of positive and negative responses as a percentage of *all* responses, not just as a percentage of respondents with opinions.
30. *Fortune* (January 1936); Cantril and Strunk, *Public Opinion*, p. 403.
31. AIPO Poll, December 13, 1937: "Do you think the cause of world peace will be hurt if the League of Nations is dissolved?"
32. See Cantril and Strunk, *Public Opinion*, p. 403.
33. For the text of the Chautauqua address and analysis of public reaction to it, see Department of State, "Public Response to President Roosevelt's Chautauqua Speech,

August 14, 1936," compiled by Shepard Jones, April 12, 1943, Bureau of Public Affairs Files, Washington, D.C.

34. For discussion of the informational activities of the State Department during the 1930s, see chapter 3 below.

35. A detailed account of these campaigns is given in chapter 4.

36. See Jonas, *Isolationism in America*, p. 17 and passim. See also Harold and Margaret Sprout, *Toward a Politics of the Planet Earth* (New York, 1971), chap. 11, for a discussion of certain geographical and cartographical misconceptions that may contribute to the feeling of isolation.

37. AIPO Poll, April 9, 1939: "If England and France go to war against Germany, do you think this country should declare war on Germany?"

38. AIPO Poll, February 16, 1939: "If Germany and Italy go to war against England and France, would it be better for the United States to help England and France or not to help either side?"

39. White's speech, "The Hour Is Striking," was broadcast on CBS radio at 1:40 P.M. "to counteract the usual Father Coughlin broadcast." It was later widely distributed on a gramaphone record. See Walter Johnson, *The Battle Against Isolation* (Chicago, 1944), p. 47.

40. AIPO Poll, September 22, 1939: "Do you think the United States will succeed in staying out of the war?" The uncertainty and lack of confidence underlying respondents' predictions are suggested by the responses to another question in the same poll. When asked, "Do you think the United States will go into the war before it is over?" respondents were less confident about America's insulation: "yes," 56 percent, "no," 44 percent. This uncertainty is underlined by the high percentage holding no opinion: 26 percent for both questions. The sensitivity of respondents to a slight change in wording emphasizes the wishful element among the 60 percent who said they still believed in the possibility of noninvolvement.

41. *Fortune* (November, 1939). "Which of these courses of action comes closest to describing what you think the United States should do (about the current European War)?" The quoted response was selected by 37 percent; the next most popular policy was "refuse aid of any kind to either side and refuse to sell anything at all to either side." (24 percent). For other responses and marginals see Cantril and Strunk, *Public Opinion*, p. 969.

42. See Johnson, *The Battle Against Isolation*, chap. 2, for details of organization and financing of the campaign to replace the arms embargo with a cash and carry scheme.

43. See ibid., p. 91, for discussion of relationship between President Roosevelt and the Committee to Defend America by Aiding the Allies.

44. White to Roosevelt, June 10, 1940, in ibid., p. 82.

3

The impact of war

WAR AND OPINION MANAGEMENT

"Government management of opinion is an unescapable corollary of large scale modern war," Harold Lasswell wrote in 1927, following a study of Woodrow Wilson's approach to domestic information policy in wartime.[1] The approach had been forthright and determined: President Wilson created a new bureaucracy with authority to analyze opinion, centralize the dissemination of information, and, if necessary, impose censorship.[2] In terms of the model outlined in chapter 1, Lasswell was pointing to an intensification of the opinion-policy relationship brought about by strengthening the linkages between the public and the government.

An intensification of the relationship can be predicted whenever policy makers have adopted, or wish to adopt, a policy that threatens shared images. The probability of public involvement is increased if the policy encroaches on vested interests, affects everyday life, and is readily comprehensible. These conditions are fulfilled most clearly in a decision to go to war. Avoidance of war is an objective that might seem almost as pressing, but this depends on the policies adopted to preserve the peace. If these policies consist in maintaining or reinforcing an existing posture, as was the case with neutrality after 1935, there is little need to elicit fresh demonstrations of public support. But if avoidance of war entails a decisive reorientation in policy, the government will seek to mobilize consent. The closer the decision comes to the "unique" end of the continuum, "the larger the role which public opinion *can* play in the policy making process."[3]

Whether public opinion actually intervenes in the process is, of course, another question. Had Lasswell been writing twenty years later he might have wished to qualify his observation; for World War II showed that though government management of opinion may be a desired objective, as an adjunct to military and psychological warfare, the objective is not always attained. The management of opinion requires new specialized machinery; in World War I it was the Committee on Public Information, in World War II, the Office of War Information, inter alia. The creation of such machinery can produce sufficient tensions with established parts of the bureaucracy and the Congress to thwart its purpose or mission.

According to Morton Halperin and Arnold Kanter, "Organizations with missions strive to maintain their (1) essential role, (2) domain, (3) autonomy, and (4) morale."[4] When a new organization is created, especially one with the vital mission of mediating between top policy makers and the public, other organizations naturally regard all four of their objectives as threatened. "Autonomy," for example, "refers to the desire of an organization to have control over its own resources in order to preserve what it views as its essence and to protect its domain from encroachment." If policy makers construe public opinion in elite terms and are content to operate through congressional intermediaries, then legislative "autonomy" will not be threatened. But if a new opinion-information bureaucracy seeks out vox populi in mass opinion, bypassing the Congress, then legislators will feel their own mission as spokesmen for that opinion to be jeopardized, and they will withhold cooperation. Because of the need for yearly appropriations from the Congress, such action can prove fatal to the new organization.

Similarly, if a new organization injects itself into the opinion-policy relationship, claiming special competence to advise policy makers on impending decisions, old "line" agencies and departments will feel their mission to be threatened. This need not prejudice the effectiveness of the new organization if its members are adept at the bureaucratic game and if the president is behind them. But if the game is bungled or the president loses interest, the outcome is likely to benefit entrenched organizations.

If the new organization's mission is restricted to the promotion of national unity or a common war effort, an acquiescent attitude on the part of the legislature may be expected, although other executive agencies may fear for their domain. But it is in the nature of a party political system, particularly one based on separation of powers, for the opposition to detect motives other than the common cause in the establishment of a direct line between the executive and public opinion. Public opinion, under another hat, is the electorate.

Such suspicions do not necessarily reflect the subordination of national to partisan goals on either side. As Lasswell remarks, when the government is involved in promotional, propaganda, or educational activities, "the line of distinction between a private advantage which is incidental to a legitimate public advantage and a private advantage which brings no overwhelming public advantage is difficult to draw.[5] But if partisan spirit is strong the natural ambiguity in governnment promotional activities is likely to be interpreted in the worst light. This occurred in 1943 when Congress severed many of the ties that had been established between the executive and the public. It did this by fatally weakening the domestic branch of the Office of War Information.

In examining this crisis we shall seek to determine which of its elements were peculiar to the circumstances of 1943 and which have a more general application. Comparison with the American experience in World War I suggests that an intensification of the opinion-policy relationship has certain implications for legislative-executive relations that transcend historical particularities. The outcome, however, depends on the style of national leadership, the disposition of power in Congress, relations with the press, and the comparative skill of the different bureaucratic players.[6]

After the demise of OWI as a link in the opinion-information-policy cycle the Office of Public Affairs in the State Department took over some of its personnel and methods. This newcomer survived long enough to play a critical role in two important decisions that shaped the pattern of international relations in the postwar period: the American decision to sponsor and join the United Nations Organization and the decision to replace Britain as the guarantor of a noncommunist Greece and Turkey. After 1947 the Office of Public Affairs ceased to be of any significance in the opinion-policy relationship. Our analysis of the intensified opinion-policy relationship in World War II serves as a bridge between the faltering public stance of the administration in the 1930s, during the expansion of fascism and the more positive orientation in the 1940s, during the expansion of communism.

A better understanding of the impact of war on the opinion-policy relationship obviates the need to rely on temperamental differences to explain the distinct approaches of Presidents Roosevelt and Truman. While personality cannot be ignored it should, perhaps, be treated as a residual whose influence is felt within bureaucratic and political constraints. Only when these constraints have been identified are we in a position to evaluate the significance of personality in the pattern of leadership.[7]

OPINION MANAGEMENT BEFORE WORLD WAR II

The advent of war in 1917 was the catalyst that first precipitated the American government into full-scale informational activities at home. It clearly fulfilled the condition of a decisive reorientation in the country's foreign policy. The condition was, in fact, "overfulfilled," inasmuch as Woodrow Wilson could accept America's belligerency only on grounds of high principle. These grounds, embodied in his Fourteen Points, had to be understood by the American people, Wilson felt, if they were to endorse so dramatic a departure from the previous policy of neutrality.[8]

As soon as the United States declared war Secretary of State Robert Lansing moved to strengthen the Division of Information, which had been set up in his department under President Taft in 1909. The releases and other publicity materials the division prepared were aimed not at the mass public but at the groups Almond calls "the policy and opinion elites." The audience of the Division of Information was limited because its meager resources promised to be most effective if aimed at those who were both opinion holders and opinion makers.[9]

Lansing, together with the secretaries of the navy and of war, advised Wilson to follow the example of other belligerents by setting up a more ambitious "Committee on Public Information." The secretaries said that the committee, on which they offered to serve, could combine with "honesty and with profit" the functions of censorship and publicity.[10] Wilson issued the necessary executive order on April 13, 1917.

The primary purpose of the Committee on Public Information (CPI) "was to sell the war to the American people and to make the American public understand and appreciate the sacrifices that would have to be made if democracy was to survive."[11] It undertook this task by monitoring the system of voluntary censorship observed by the press and by sponsoring many independent publicity campaigns of its own. The organizational structure of the committee was less well defined than that of its successors in World War II, but it was divided broadly into domestic and foreign sections. At home the committee had bureaus that issued news releases, published an *Official Bulletin*, produced and distributed films, mounted exhibitions on war themes, arranged advertising, prepared posters and cartoons, and dispatched "Four Minute Men" around the country to give brief talks before the show in movies and theaters on themes currently being developed by the committee. It also addressed its literature to specific groups, including the foreign born, women's organizations, business, and labor.[12]

These activities linked the government wih the public through the diffusion of information. It took the form of an avowed campaign of education and persuasion dealing not only with the war itself but with "the Wilson program of reconstruction." At this time no mechanism existed for assessing public opinion systematically.

The flow of information was predominantly from the government to the public. The CPI did not "transmit" or "submit" articulated opinion to policy makers in the manner of later public-opinion experts. Public opinion was important as the *object* of government activity, not as an input into decision making. George Creel, chairman of the CPI, thought in terms of the manipulation of symbols that could readily be associated with Wilson's Fourteen Points or their Manichean opposites.

Three characteristics of the committee distinguished it most clearly from its World War II successor, OWI. (1) It virtually ignored the transmission of opinion to policy makers, concentrating on the diffusion of information to the public. (2) It exercised the function of censorship. (3) Its organizational structure included three leaders of enormous prestige, the cabinet secretaries who proposed the scheme to Wilson. Because of their own stake in the committee, the Departments of State, War, and Navy did not feel that their autonomy was threatened. They cooperated in centralizing the diffusion of information.

But the committee did seek to establish a direct line to public opinion, albeit a line with predominantly one-way transmission. This seemed to many congressmen like an encroachment on their "essential role." George Creel was charged with disloyalty and with undue political partisanship by opponents of the Administration. Creel was accused of boosting Woodrow Wilson's image for domestic political reasons and of suborning the press. He was abused by senators and congressmen, in terms similar to the following attack by Senator Boies Penrose of Pennsylvania, under the shield of their immunity,

> I do not see why we should permit men like Mr. Creel for instance, whose scurrilous and defamatory utterances on the Constitution of the United States were read in this body the other day, to be holding an office and publishing a publicity chronicle, when he is smeared all over with treason. [13]

Creel had had a long career as a newspaperman, a Wilson supporter, and a publicist so the attacks, however exaggerated, were scarcely surprising. "The selection of such a man," Lasswell observes, "is certain to arouse nasty insinuations in the legislature." [14]

The particular flavor of these insinuations may have been supplied by Creel's often abrasive advocacy of Wilson's policies. But their origins lie in the intensification of the opinion-policy relationship; for unless war succeeds in permeating the legislature with an exceptional degree of nonpartisanship, executive intervention in the information field leads ineluctably to legislative-executive tensions. Such nonpartisanship is rarely achieved even in countries, such as Britain, where wartime governments of national unity have been formed.

One of the most potent national symbols available to information officers is the chief executive, but the chief executive is also a party leader. Lloyd George, as well as Wilson and Franklin Roosevelt, earned the condemnation of elected representatives of the opposition party by lending their names, exploits, and pictures to campaigns ostensibly serving the public purpose. [15]

Legislative assaults can make little headway as long as their objects continue to enjoy the confidence of the president. But when that support is withdrawn they can lead to the elimination of the agencies involved. This happened to OWI's domestic operations in 1943. Two decades later in 1957 the State Department's Public Studies Division was liquidated at the behest of Congress after the president, the secretary of state, and even the assistant secretary for public affairs had lost interest in its existence.

In 1917, the press added to the congressional assault on Creel's organization. By taking on the job of press censorship the CPI earned the resentment of the fourth branch. Creel's own abrasive personality invited further attack. In World War II the OWI was denied any role in censorship. This complicated its task of coordination but at least kept it on good terms with the press, for whom it provided a useful service. Many newspapers defended Elmer Davis's organization, perhaps saving OWI's domestic branch from complete annihilation.

THE INTERWAR PERIOD

In the 1920s and 1930s many long-established government departments became concerned with publicity and information. Informational activities received a tremendous boost from the New Deal. The United States Information Service was set up to inform the public about their rights under the new social security legislation. "Each of the old-line departments established informational units or bureaus. Because of Congressional dislike of the terms 'publicity and public relations' within a Federal Department or agency, 'information unit' was the mask under which public relations activities were established."[16]

The Department of Agriculture was in the forefront of information work during the interwar years. Its activities would have no particular significance for our understanding of the impact of war on the opinion-foreign policy relationship were it not for the fact that by 1929 Milton Eisenhower had taken over as director of the department's Office of Information. The techniques Eisenhower developed in this capacity provided the basis for a report he submitted to the Budget Bureau in 1942 recommending the establishment of a Committee on War Information.[17] This report was one of the two memoranda that led to the establishment of OWI; Eisenhower was later appointed to OWI's domestic branch.

Eisenhower's annual report as director of information at Agriculture in 1929 helps to distinguish interwar from wartime information activities. "The Office of Information," he wrote,

is in no wise a publicity agency in the usual sense of that term. Its purpose is not to acquire prestige for itself or for the Department as a whole, not to "sell" the Department to the public or to advertise the achievements of Department workers, but to make public the results of the Department's manifold activities.[18]

Allowing for a certain amount of prudent modesty, this statement explains the nonabrasive quality of interwar information work. Apart from the strictly functional nature of most of the information disseminated (many farmers quite genuinely sought information from the Department of Agriculture) the federal government spoke through many offices. It did not threaten the traditional prerogatives of Congress or the press.

At this time the State Department enjoyed only limited access to the process of foreign-policy decision making. This process itself was somewhat atrophied in the early 1930s when the administration was largely devoted to the national recovery program at home. The president's diplomacy operated within the confines of isolationism and, after 1935, neutrality. The State Department's response to the mounting depredations of Japan stuck at the doctrine of nonrecognition, to the exasperation of officers in the field, like Joseph Stilwell, who advocated intervention on China's behalf.

The only exception to this highly introverted approach was Roosevelt's decision in 1933 to recognize the Soviet Union. [19] Even this decision was made largely on economic grounds in response to the urgings of labor and business organizations, impressed by Stalin's first Five Year Plan, the Soviet Union's apparent immunity to the depression, and the many economic opportunities the Soviet Union seemed to offer to Americans. In the public debate preceding recognition proponents of the move grossly exaggerated the prospects of trade with the U.S.S.R. and, often unconsciously, distorted the character of the Soviet regime. [20] Opinion groups were reinforced by the press; the Scripps-Howard group, for example, boldly advocated recognition. [21]

In this case public opinion intervened at the first stage of the decision process; [22] it performed an agenda-setting function by holding the issue salient for Roosevelt, leading to recognition and resumption of diplomatic relations.

As compensation for his virtual exclusion from the formulation of "high" policy concerning national security, foreign economic policy became almost exclusively the preserve of Secretary Hull. In chapter 2 we referred to Hull's extreme sensitivity to isolationist opinion. He was generally reluctant to gainsay this opinion in military or diplomatic policy but not in the matter of free trade. [23] Here the going was easier for very few isolationists believed in the isolation of American trade. The task, in Hull's view, was to gain acceptance for his plan to replace the old, restrictive Smoot-Hawley tariff by a system of reciprocal trade agreements. This project had an important effect on the development of linkages between the foreign-policy bureaucracy and public opinion. As one participant in the public-information campaign boosting the plan later observed: "If there is any single point dividing the old from the new in the evolution of the Department of State's relationship to the American people it is the Trade Agreements Act of 1934. New foreign policies involving established domestic interests brought new information practices." [24]

Francis B. Sayre was the assistant secretary of state responsible for trade agreements. (He was also chairman of the president's Executive Committee on Commercial Policy and, incidently, a son-in-law of Woodrow Wilson.) His office undertook a public strategy designed to win support for the trade agreements bill from farm, labor, and other domestic interests. The decisive change signalled by this strategy was the conviction that it was necessary for the State Department to educate the American people and to establish a close liaison with their representatives.

Accordingly, the Economic Policy Committee drew up a memorandum, "Program for Trade Agreements Education," which began by noting that "the need for sound educational activity in the field of foreign trade policy is greater today than at any time." [25] It called for a leaflet campaign addressed to the mass public. Leaflets were considered "the most effective medium in the literature field. Lengthy brochures are needed for leaders training, but not in popular education." A poll of economists was organized, not so much to test the wisdom of the program, a foregone conclusion, but to elicit a plurality of support, which could then be used for further publicity. The campaign also provided for liaison with farm and business groups and radio broadcasts to reach the general public. A "Foreign Trade Week" was sponsored in New York City, heralded by a talk on WNYC radio by Dr. Paul V. Horn entitled, "Foreign Trade and Your Sunday Dinner." In the program, which was broadcast at 12:30 P.M. on Sunday May 19, Dr. Horn took his listeners on an excursion around their dinner table pointing out the foreign origins of their favorite foods and seasonings. [26]

The general public was a target of "education" only to the extent that its approval was needed to reassure congressmen that they might safely embark on the new course. Sayre's strategy was aimed at the "policy and opinion elite" in general and economic groups in particular. The formula was so successful that it was repeated in 1937, 1940, and 1943 when the trade agreements came up for renewal.

From this experience "the Department of State not only learned more about keeping the public informed; it also began to learn about keeping itself informed about the public."[27] After 1939 it was able to do this, not only by direct contact with interested parties, but also with the aid of public-opinion polls. It became part of the ethic of publicity men in the State Department that their relationship with the public ought to be a two-way street. One-sided lectures were both ineffective and offensive. They were likely to reawaken the suspicions of the Congress, never long dormant. The public had to be consulted if it were to be persuaded.[28]

These developments were more significant in the long-term evolution of the opinion-policy relationship than in the political context of the 1930s. Hull's range of activities was sharply limited. Except for the periodic renewals of the Trade Agreements, State Department involvement with the American public dwindled to insignificance for almost a decade. "Traditional foreign office ways continued to dominate the handling of our international political affairs."[29] Hull brooded over his apparent impotence in face of the "irreconcilables" in Congress, who clung to the arms embargo and to their peculiar brand of pacifism. "Foreign policy must necessarily rest upon an informed and united *public opinion,*" he noted. "In no other way can the democratic process function. If public opinion is divided in many directions with respect to basic conditions in our international affairs and basic programs for dealing with the same, our government has little or no moral influence for good in world capitals, but its foreign policy is more or less a failure and so recognized in every foreign capital."[30] While windows had been opened in foreign economic policy the Nye committee had slammed them closed in the more vital sphere of diplomatic and military policy.

Despite the malaise reflected in Hull's notes the flurry of promotional activity in the 1930s was not without an indirect influence on future foreign relations. State Department officers, like John Sloan Dickey, who received their first exposure to "opinion making" in this rather narrow sphere later applied similar techniques during more fundamental shifts in America's foreign policy, notably its sponsorship of the United Nations. But, for the moment, the task of creating that "informed and united public opinion" did not fall to the State Department.

In fact, it fell to no single organization to tackle the divisions in public opinion. This reflected the president's predilection for a multiplicity of agencies with overlapping functions, each relying on the White House rather than on an established executive department for its authority. Although Roosevelt himself was slow to seize the opinion-making initiative, many government agencies acquired their own outlets to the public. "As the European crisis increased the information units of the War and Navy Departments increased enormously," as did those of the network of agencies created by authority of the Council of National Defense in 1940.[31]

THE OUTBREAK OF WAR

Great Britain entered World War II on September 3, 1939. Although by this time public opinion in America was less resolutely isolationist (and perhaps more open to persuasion) than Roosevelt and Hull believed, the administration still faced a wall of isolationism among the old "irreconcilables" in the Senate. The delicacy of the parliamentary situation, coupled with Roosevelt's lingering vulnerability after the Supreme Court fight, gave him the uncomfortable sensation of "walking on eggs."[32] So, even when the administration decided to take the offensive and fight for repeal of the arms embargo, it did so not by seeking to influence public opinion directly but through the intermediary of the Non-Partisan Committee for Peace through the Revision of the Neutrality Law, headed by William Allen White, the Republican editor of the *Emporia Gazette*. The agitation of the White committee was successful, and the arms embargo was repealed in the Senate by 63 to 30 and in the House by 243 to 181.

After this first decisive break with the most egregious feature of the Neutrality Act, the administration ventured more boldly into the field of public-information campaigns. It again relied on the White committee, now called the Committee to Defend America by Aiding the Allies, to persuade Congress of the necessity of lend-lease and convoys. But, at the same time, a new network of agencies designed to inform and influence opinion was coalescing under the Office of Emergency Management and the Council of National Defense. This council was set up in 1940, by authority of the 1916 National Defense Act, to coordinate government reaction to the fast developing international crisis.

Five days after the outbreak of war in Europe the president issued an executive order establishing the Office of Government Reports (OGR) as an administrative unit within the executive office of the president. Two clauses in the executive order indicated that OGR was to function both as a disseminator of information to the public and as a transmitter of opinion to the president. The OGR was

to collect and distribute information concerning the purposes and activities of executive departments and agencies for the use of the Congress, administrative officials and the public;

and,

to keep the President currently informed of the opinions, desires and complaints of citizens and groups of citizens and of state and local governments with respect to the work of federal agencies. [33]

To perform these functions OGR took over the facilities of two New Deal agencies, the Division of Press Intelligence (DPI) and the United States Information Service (USIS), which had been established in 1933 and 1934, respectively. These agencies had been set up during the depression to inform the government about press reaction to the national recovery program and to inform the people about the New Deal. As part of OGR, the content of the information they handled would reflect the altered character of the national emergency, one that came to stress national defense as the international situation deteriorated.

Public opinion would also be submitted to the White House by OGR's Division of Field Operations, whose network of representatives across the United States reported local sentiment. Although unscientific by comparison with the public-opinion polls that were trickling into the White House by 1939, field reports were valued for their ability to capture nuance. Indeed throughout this period pollsters found it difficult to wrest presidential attention from more colorful sources of opinion.

OGR's scope was limited; it had far less authority than the old Creel committee. Its director, Lowell Mellett, former editor of the *Washington Daily News* and an assistant to the president, eschewed the kind of "great educational campaigns" advocated by other presidential advisers. [34] Mellett's conception of his office was a modest one, a neutral intermediary between the government and the public. Because of Mellett's conception OGR could never become an authoritative instrument of national preparedness while so many other government information agencies were in competition for public attention.

The president reassured Congressman O'Leary, chairman of the House Committee on Expenditures in the Executive Departments, that he intended to create no superbureau but only a "clearing house for information" and a channel for relaying public opinion to the president. [35] It could even be argued that the Constitution required the president to gauge public opinion in order that he might carry out his duty to report on the state of the nation.

Despite these many disclaimers, the bureaucratic pedigree of OGR guaranteed the hostility of anti-New Deal congressmen. OGR excited legislative fears of censorship and propaganda, forcing Mellett to issue frequent denials both in print and in testimony on Capitol Hill. By 1941 Mellett felt himself to be in a double bind. "I am weary of being charged with engaging in propaganda, on the one hand, and weary of being urged to engage in propaganda on the other," he wrote. [36] Peacetime propaganda was not the American way:

> It would be wrong of the President to use funds voted by Congress to set up an agency designed to whip Congress into line with his thinking. And the President has not done so. It would be wrong and it would be unwise, since national policy is always in the process of making and the collaboration of President and Congress is always essential. [37]

Rather more pragmatically, Mellett told the readers of *The Atlantic Monthly* that propaganda would be unnecessary, since the public had accepted conscription "without batting an eyelid," and lend-lease had fared no worse.

The lightly veiled innuendo in Mellett's article was addressed to a group of presidential friends and advisers who did not share his own confidence in continuing public support for emergency measures. To Harold Ickes, Dean Acheson, William Bullitt, and Archibald MacLeish the fall of France and isolation of Great Britain carried grave portents for the United States. The situation, they thought, warranted something more than Mellett's complacency concerning public-information policy. Even during the struggle for repeal of the arms embargo they had counseled a more vigorous public presentation of the threat posed by Axis aggression. At the time Roosevelt had temporized because of the precarious balance in Congress; but by 1941 this "walking on eggs" phase had passed and his advisers pressed for something more authoritative than Mellett's organization. OGR scarcely satisfied Ickes's insistence that it was "vitally important to educate our own people on the issues involved."[38]

When the Council of National Defense, defunct since World War I, was reestablished in May 1940 the president moved to create an information agency with wider powers. It would be a "recreation," on a very limited scale, of the Creel Committee and to some extent an adaptation of the kind of information agency existing in the Axis dictatorships."[39] The new agency, to be called the Division of Information (DOI), would mediate between the network of bureaus that had grown out of the Office of Emergency Management (OEM) and the public.

The orientation of the new agency was to be altogether more activist than its predecessors. Robert Horton, a former editor for the Scripps-Howard group of newspapers, which had supported Roosevelt's decision to recognize the Soviet Union in 1933, was selected as director. "Horton believed in an aggressive *opinion-influencing* agency which would put forth the information which the government desired the public to have."[40] Its responsibilities extended coordination to the development of material for movies, radio, and the press.

Despite these intentions the division never came to exercise fully those functions for which it had been designed. It competed for media attention with units in the Treasury, the armed services, and other government departments. "The existence of competing informational units which refused to recognize DOI's authority plus the indisposition of President Roosevelt to assign the central information work to Horton, were major factors in the growing confusion regarding Federal information."[41]

Roosevelt's hesitancy owed something to the style of his leadership, but he was also influenced by lingering congressional suspicions. The "irreconcilables" in the Senate were convinced that any move to centralize the government's information services would be tantamount to enlisting the public on the side of war.

In addition to OGR and DOI, several other agencies put themselves forward as candidates for the central position in any new superagency; they included Mayor La Guardia's Office of Civilian Defense (OCD), Robert Sherwood's Foreign Information Service (FIS), and "Wild Bill"

Donovan's Office of the Co-ordinator of Information (COI). Bureau-cratic interests and personal rivalries added to the delay in rationalizing the machinery for the diffusion of defense information to the public.

There was no shortage of suggestions concerning the leadership, struc-ture, and functions of a new superagency. Early in 1941 the president considered the possibility of bringing back George Creel to organize another Committee on Public Information along the lines of the World War I organization. But Harold Ickes reminded Roosevelt of the number of people who had been antagonized by the first Creel operation. Some-one less abrasive was needed.[42]

The first serious candidate for the role of "saviour" was the somewhat facetiously named Office of Facts and Figures (OFF). An organization by that name was first established within Mayor La Guardia's Office of Civilian Defense. It did not attempt an extensive survey research pro-gram, concentrating instead on coordinating government radio pro-grams and disseminating information about defense work to the press.

The operation soon found itself hampered not only by its limited authority but by La Guardia's administrative methods. The mayor was unwilling to direct the work himself and was temperamentally incapable of delegating authority.[43] Robert Kintner, the columnist, then working in OFF, prepared a memorandum for the Budget Bureau recommend-ing the establishment of a separate OFF under the auspices of the Office of Emergency Management. This proposal pleased the set of presi-dential advisers and assistants who were dissatisfied with the disarray in the information field. Judge Samuel Rosenman, Roosevelt's close per-sonal assistant, took Kintner's proposal up with the president and was authorized to prepare an executive order. At the suggestion of Rosen-man, the White House contacted Archibald MacLeish, the poet and Librarian of Congress, about directing the organization. MacLeish was enthusiastic about the idea and indicated that he had in mind a policy role that transcended the rather limited public-relations work conducted by his predecessors.[44]

President Roosevelt signed the executive order on October 24, 1941, scarcely more than six weeks before the attack on Pearl Harbor. Its terms did not provide for a new Creel operation; government departments were to continue to handle their own publicity. OFF's functions included co-ordination, but not the kind of mandatory clearance exercised during World War I.

After receiving notice of his appointment MacLeish wrote to Harry

Hopkins that his job was "one of co-ordination, not of control or regulation."[45] This job, he hoped, would not arouse criticism of censorship in a democracy but would give him the authority to affect high-level decision making by virtue of the information at his disposal. MacLeish's aspiration followed the good bureaucratic principle that the person who is well briefed will prevail.

The limited function of coordination suited MacLeish temperamentally and appealed to him on ideological grounds. Having abandoned the pacifism of his early interwar years, the poet now interpreted the world crisis as a struggle between democracy and totalitarianism. It seemed to him fitting that in a democracy the government should "take the people into [its] confidence" without imposing the kind of controls totalitarians employed. Very soon he was to discover that bureaucratic pressures demanded that he assume more authority if OFF were to bring order and clarity to the information scene.

Two features of OFF's brief history pointed to a more intense opinion-policy relationship. First, the attack on Pearl Harbor added a counter-propaganda function and increased the urgency of OFF's task. Second, MacLeish seized the opportunity to set up an elaborate public-opinion survey organization. The Bureau of Intelligence was OFF's most important innovation in the opinion-policy field.[46] It survived the demise of OFF to become incorporated in the OWI. The "OWI Study" assesses its importance as follows:

> The Bureau of Intelligence, while not the first government organization dealing with surveys of American opinion, was the first federal effort to judge overall American opinion. The Bureau of Intelligence, mainly following the technique of market research and the Gallup poll technique, attempted to discover the issues on which the American public desired information or those on which it was falsely informed. It also developed a system to pre-test government campaigns and program material in order to determine whether the public reached reacted to this material in the manner the government desired.

The bureau consumed the largest share of OFF's funds and, by June 1942, employed 126 people on the analysis of public opinion. In addition 160 people were engaged on OFF assignments in the Surveys Division of the Department of Agriculture. The Bureau of Intelligence was also the normal conduit to the president for data gathered and analyzed by Hadley Cantril's Office of Public Opinion Research at Princeton.

The scientific nature of the bureau's reports gave MacLeish the edge on other would-be submitters of popular opinion, such as Mellett who relied on field reports. In fact, "the information collected by the Bureau of Intelligence was used by MacLeish as his special entrée to the White House."[47] He also had the advantage of personal friendship with the president from his days as Librarian of Congress, when the MacLeishes would visit the president at Shangri La. He was on friendly terms with Anna Rosenberg, Harry Hopkins, Roosevelt's close political aide, and Stephen Early, the president's press secretary.

"The strategy of truth" became the slogan of home-front information work and, to a slightly lesser extent, of propaganda directed abroad. A separate Office of Censorship had been set up (a further distinction from the Creel operation) so MacLeish hoped to be spared the brunt of press criticism.[48]

Unfortunately, the strategy of truth guaranteed no such immunity. Despite brave efforts to profit from the negative example of the Creel committee, OFF soon encountered withering criticism from the press. Although most editorial writers accepted Roosevelt's criteria for the dissemination of information, many felt that these criteria were misapplied, with blackouts applied to information of no strategic value to the enemy.

Columnists, basically sympathetic to the administration's war aims, complained about the "sugar-coated" releases OFF issued. To imbue a false sense of confidence was to repeat the error of the British before Dunkirk. James Reston of the *New York Times* wrote: "The officials charged with the dissemination of our war information have not yet learned one of the most fundamental psychological lessons of the war, that the Anglo-Saxon peoples will not make the revolutionary sacrifices now necessary until they understand that the position of their countries in the war is desperate."[49] Similar observations, based on poll data, reached the White House through the Bureau of Intelligence. Hadley Cantril repeatedly told Roosevelt that tremendous sacrifice would be forthcoming if only the administration gave strong leadership and did not hide harsh realities.[50]

MacLeish concurred in Cantril's judgment, but he and his assistants did not have the mechanisms at their disposal to coordinate a national appeal. OFF was in the anomalous position of having the authority to edit the speeches of cabinet members but not to tone down the over-optimistic press releases from service departments. The result was that in February 1942 the public received a very confused picture of the war. EFFORTS TO HARMONIZE FACTS AND FIGURES HAVE NOT YET SUCCEEDED, announced the headline to Reston's story.

The *New York Times'* criticisms were at least offered in a constructive spirit. But the attacks on OFF from the Midwest and from those not yet reconciled to the breakdown of isolationism were more scurrilous. The *Chicago Tribune* (May 13, 1942) complained that OFF paid its employees inflated salaries.[51] Other newspapers picked on MacLeish as too committed an exponent of the government's foreign policy, which the isolationist press viewed as an attempt to internationalize the New Deal. MacLeish's criticisms of Roosevelt's opponents could not be easily overlooked in an election year.

Both the controversial Librarian of Congress and the structure of OFF began to appear as a liability to Roosevelt. MacLeish was no less frustrated by the situation. The problem, he came to believe, went right back to the executive order that Rosenman had drafted. In its zeal to avoid the appearance of harsh controls, the order left OFF with insufficient authority to coordinate the output of the many agencies in the information business. This was an organic defeat of such magnitude that after only four months of operation MacLeish recommended the liquidation of OFF and the incorporation of its more successful innovations, notably the Bureau of Intelligence, into a new Office of War Information.[52]

The director of the Budget Bureau and his staff had entertained few illusions about OFF's prospects from its inception. It had been an interim solution before the government adjusted to the imperatives of war. Late in 1941, Budget Director Harold Smith ordered a study to be made of the government's facilities for disseminating information and analyzing public opinion. Milton Eisenhower, director of information at the Department of Agriculture, was commissioned to undertake the task.

The Budget Bureau reformers received conflicting advice from those involved in information work. Stephen Early, the president's press secretary, and Lowell Mellett, administrative assistant to the president and director of the OGR, counseled against the resurrection of a Creel type of operation. This advice reflected not only judgments based on criteria of effectiveness but also personal and bureaucratic interests. Early cherished his own rapport with the press, and Mellett wished to protect the operations of OGR, which would be absorbed into the new agency if MacLeish's advice to Smith were accepted. Ever since the establishment of OGR Mellett had battled against Ickes and others who told the president that the situation warranted a far more systematic approach to domestic opinion.

In contrast to the complacency of Early and Mellett, La Guardia, Rosenman, Hopkins, and MacLeish took a serious, if not alarmist, view of the prevailing confusion. "Government information," MacLeish thought should provide a basis for public *opinion making* and morale building." It "should be employed to strengthen, if not develop, emotions in the American people, either hatred towards the Axis or idealistic love of the Atlantic Charter and the Four Freedoms."[53] There would be little chance of evoking emotions of this intensity without a radical reform of the administrative structure.

These dissentions bubbled scarcely out of earshot of journalists who had a special interest in their outcome.

Disagreements among his advisers provided Roosevelt with a pretext to rely for the moment on the expedient offered by OFF. At his press conference on April 3, 1942, the president conceded that no agreement had been reached, although he attributed the delay to technical difficulties. He said there were a half-dozen methods for achieving the desired coordination.[54]

Eisenhower's report did not dismiss OFF entirely, finding words of praise in particular for the Bureau of Intelligence: "Through the Intelligence Bureau of OFF, the planning work has been able to take the current state of public opinion into careful consideration, and valuable clues have been furnished as to tensions and grievances that are threatening to develop."[55] But he recommended the creation of a stronger Committee on War Information to coordinate and control all the existing ad hoc organizations. Good liaison with other executive departments was essential. He envisaged a series of interdepartmental committees to provide the coordination lacking in OFF. This suggestion seemed inadequate to Bernard Gladeaux of the Budget Bureau who cast his proposal in terms of an Office of War Information, rather than a committee, with its aura of discussion and delay. A centralized structure was needed.

Both the Eisenhower and Gladeaux proposals were incorporated into the memorandum that the Budget Bureau submitted to the president. FDR did not act on the memorandum immediately; three months went by after he received it in March while the leading protagonists argued their cases. Finally an executive order was drawn up in May 1942 but the president continued to sit on it while press attacks on bureaucratic confusion mounted. Harold Smith wrote to the president pointing out that the end of the fiscal year was approaching and that unless the executive order were issued by June 30, Congress might insist on an investigation of the competing claims for appropriations.

This letter seems to have pushed the president toward decision. Budget deadlines frequently perform the function of curtailing interagency debates.[56] Roosevelt prevailed upon Elmer Davis,[57] a noted journalist, to accept the directorship and issued the executive order on June 13, 1942. Davis came strongly recommended by Harry Hopkins. The president obviously hoped to avoid anyone as controversial as MacLeish since good relations with the press and the Congress were essential conditions for success.

OWI was not a central information production agency along the lines of the Creel committee or the British Ministry of Information.[58] Yet it was an originator of news stories and of its own publications. It was expected to clear information from other agencies "which bear significantly on the war effort or war policies." This raised problems of demarcation; old-line departments were still issuing their own information, with the attendant probability of self-contradiction. The State Department was particularly jealous of its prerogatives and often differed with OWI about the information that fell into the above category.

The State Department sought to exclude itself from OWI clearance, thus, in Davis's words, "virtually nullifying Executive Order 9182."[59] Toward the end of the war a joint State Department-OWI committee was set up, but on the whole, Davis complained, "the Department cooperated with OWI only when and in so far as it chose." After the rebuff served to OWI by the Congress in 1943 (see p. 92), the president tried to demonstrate his continuing confidence in OWI by instructing Hull to cooperate more fully.[60] But by then the influence of OWI on the home front had already reached its nadir.

"It is important to give the propagandist a place, not only in the actual execution of policy, but in the formation," Lasswell argued. "Policies are not safely formulated without expert information on the state of that opinion upon which they rely for success."[61] Lasswell's prescription, based on his study of propaganda technique in World War I, remained an unattained ideal in World War II. Bureaucratic ineptitude on the part of "in and outers" like Davis, whose skills lay in journalism rather than interagency politics, diminished their influence in policy circles. Davis did not seize the initiative in establishing the authority of OWI with top policy makers. Personal contacts with presidential advisers and a "scientifically" based brief were no longer sufficient as the pressures of war mounted. The "OWI Study" points to a certain naiveté in matters of bureaucratic politics:

> Mr. Davis, in contacting department heads and other high officials of the government, too modestly refrained from insisting upon a status and a position equivalent to a Cabinet member. In view of public opinion, and in view of the President's temporary interest in the information problem it would seem that Davis might, at that time, have established himself on a level of a cabinet officer, and hence been the official equal of any person outside of the White House. Davis's failure to insist on highest level liaison caused the official mind in Washington to ignore the stature of the director of OWI, particularly after Presidential attention was turned to other problems.[62]

And presidential attention did stray from the information field after OWI had been set up. Elmer Davis was not the man to command Roosevelt's attention but his collaborator, Hadley Cantril at Princeton, did not give up. Cantril was frustrated at the thought that his efforts in gathering and transmitting public-opinion data to the White House were being wasted, so he determined to startle the president into paying attention. Cantril concluded from the polls that the public would accept greater sacrifices for the war effort if the president would only give a lead. "I have tried to make this point dozens of times," he wrote to Anna Rosenberg at the White House,

> but somehow there seems little connection between the information all of us gather and policy formation. So I resorted to a nefarious stunt and suggested to Gallup he run again his question on the President's popularity. In tomorrow's releases you will notice the President's popularity has gone down eight points.[63]

He predicted substantial Republican gains in the big states of Ohio, New York, Pennsylvania, and California. Public-opinion data showed,

VERNON REGIONAL
JUNIOR COLLEGE LIBRARY

Cantril argued, that these losses would not result from excessive demands placed upon the public but from an absence of strong leadership. "What the people want is to be told what to do," he added in capitals. It is not indicated whether the president's attention was captured by this variant of the strategy of the leak—a fascinating unique attempt to use public-opinion data coercively. But the incident itself expresses the failure of OWI regularly to incorporate its findings in high-level decision making.

THE CONTENT OF PUBLIC-OPINION RESEARCH

Hadley Cantril's informal access to the White House gave the president an opportunity not just to study the polls but to influence the choice of survey questions. Cantril told the president: "We can get confidential information on questions you suggest, follow up any hunches you may care to see tested regarding the determinants of opinion, and provide you with the answers to any questions ever asked by the Gallup or Fortune Polls. We have the only classified index of these polls in existence."[64] Cantril once went so far as to conduct a "poll" of the president in which he could express a preference for topics to appear in sample surveys. Cantril's eagerness for social science to make its contribution to wartime decision making was, at times, a source of amusement at the White House.[65] His enthusiasm reveals a purpose that did not recognize any division between national and partisan interest. This problem came up repeatedly in congressional hearings on the domestic activities of OWI.

Special Poll of the President

If you would be particularly interested in knowing public opinion on any of the following topics, please check.

___ 1. What was the reaction to Willkie's trip? Did it raise him in Presidential stature etc.?

___ 2. Has the President shown a firmer hand on war measures lately? If so, do people approve or disapprove?

___ 3. Do people understand fully the reasons for the delayed announcement of our naval losses? If not, where do they place the blame? Are they suspicious?

___ 4a. What are the major reasons for American criticism of the British?

     b. After above is completed a special study could be designed to learn the most convincing measures that might be taken either by us or by the British to forestall and correct major criticisms.

___ 5. Should a second front be left up to military leaders or should everyone express his opinion? On the second front issue, are people patient, frustrated, confident, anxious, or what?

___ 6. (Anything else)

Hadley Cantril   *October 27, 1942*

Source: "The Wartime Notebooks of Hadley Cantril," vol. 1, Roper Center, Williams College.

Despite the scientific basis of the polls themselves it could not be said that they were transmitted without special pleading. MacLeish used the polls as "his special entrée" to the White House and was an important member of the interventionist faction among the president's advisers, both in the military and the "home front" context. The same was true of Cantril, who assumed that the president needed the authority of an approving body of the public opinion to sustain him in each measure of assistance to Britain and the U.S.S.R.

But did the exhortations accompanying the submission of opinion data have any impact on presidential decisions? The researcher is often frustrated by the president's unwillingness to discuss the importance he attached to opinion data. Often the nearest we can come to empirical verification of the hypothesis that opinion submitted to the president influenced his choice of policy is the observation of a conjunction between the submission of opinion data and some new initiative.

A case in point occurred in May 1941. Responses to nine questions in a Gallup poll were submitted to the president. These responses showed an overwhelming, though diminishing, majority opposed to a decision to enter the war with Germany and Italy. Substantial majorities, however, favored more assistance for Britain. The final five items on the report sent to the president are shown in table 6. In addition to these rather

TABLE 6
Interventionism, 1941

Would you rather see Britain surrender to Germany than have the United States go into war?

Would rather see Britain surrender	26%
No opinion	12
Would rather have United States go into war	62

Should the United States Navy be used to guard ships carrying war materials to Britain?

Yes	54%
No	39
No opinion	7

If it appears certain to you that Britain will be defeated unless we use part of our navy to protect ships going to Britain would you favor or oppose such convoys?

Favor	73%
Oppose	23
No opinion	4

Do you think if our navy guards ships carrying materials to Britain, this will get us into the war?

Yes	74%
No	16%
No opinion	10%

Some people say that if the United States goes on helping England, Germany may start a war against our country. Do you think we should continue helping England, even if we run this risk?

Yes	76%
No	21
No opinion	3

Source: Memorandum, Cantril to Rosenberg, conveying data based on a Gallup survey conducted between May 7 and May 17, 1941, President's Secretary's Files, 173, Franklin D. Roosevelt Library.

specific questions, with their relentlessly interventionist logic, respondents were asked whether Roosevelt had gone too far or not far enough in helping Britain. Nineteen percent thought that he had gone too far, 53 percent thought his policy about right, while 18 percent thought he had not gone far enough. With respect to this particular finding Cantril offered the following analysis and advice to the White House:

> Since the *general* point of view of the country is for all out aid and since the President's popularity is still at an all time high (around 72%) and since people are never very clear about *specific* ways to instrument their general attitudes, I would bet anything that should the President come out for convoys or other specific aid that one week later about the same result would be found on [the above question]. At least half the population will follow him whatever he does, at least 15% will be ahead of him, at least 15% would disagree with him. [66]

Shortly after receiving this counsel to proceed in the confidence of public approval of any further step toward involvement the president gave a radio address. In it he proclaimed "an unlimited national emergency" and pledged full-scale support for Britain. "All additional measures necessary to deliver the goods will be taken." "The delivery of necessary supplies to Britain is imperative," and, he added sonorously; "This can be done; it must be done; it will be done." [67]

Public reaction to this speech was immediate and overwhelmingly favorable. The telegrams were 95 percent favorable, "and I figured I'd be lucky to get an even break on the speech," Roosevelt told Robert Sherwood who became head of the overseas branch of OWI. [68] The press was no less sympathetic. Yet, as in the case of the 1937 quarantine speech, to which the reaction had been very mixed, the president backed away from his own boldness and admitted to the press that neither convoys nor an attempt to repeal the Neutrality Act was envisaged.

Clearly public support was a necessary but not a sufficient condition for a decisive move. The constraints that delayed the move from May until September cannot fairly be said to have inhered in public opinion. Sensitivity to congressional isolationism continued to be a factor, although with such clear public pluralities for decisive action the obstacle was not insurmountable. As commander-in-chief the president had the necessary authority for the proposed initiative, but he was restrained by his own disinclination. "I am waiting to be pushed into the situation," he told Henry Morgenthau in mid-May."[69]

The White House asked Princeton for an appraisal of the public reaction to the president's May 27 radio speech. Roosevelt seemed puzzled because the immediate favorable reaction had not been sustained. Cantril's reply contained a mixture of analysis and what he called "editorializing":

> The main reason why it [the speech] had comparatively little effect was that he [the president] failed to indicate any new, overt policy that people could readily conceptualize, and that "national emergency" meant little when it required no change whatever in daily life.[70]

The majority already favored convoys to protect Atlantic shipping and so must have wondered why convoying, which the president deemed to be vital, had not begun.

The Princeton office followed up on the White House enquiry by doing a study of the variation in interventionism among those who did and did not listen to presidential radio addresses. In general listening to presidential speeches was found to vary directly with income level (see table 7). Normally the Princeton studies had shown a tendency for interventionism to vary directly with income level also. The September study confirmed this tendency but with the qualification that those who listened to the president's talks tended to be more interventionist at all economic levels. On the question of aid to Britain at the risk of getting into the war, the people in the lowest economic group who listened were more interventionist than those in the highest group who did not listen. The rank order of interventionist opinion on this question is shown in table 8. This result was not a quirk of the particular question or its wording. Other indicators of isolationism produced similar results. The tendency of individuals to feel that they would be affected by German victory over England varied with economic status. The lower-income group generally felt themselves to be least affected by such a contingency. But people who listened to the president's radio addresses felt themselves to be more involved in the consequences of German victory than people who did not listen, irrespective of economic status.[71]

Studies made before and after fireside chats revealed a pattern of strong immediate impact followed by a slipping away back to former

TABLE 7
Did You Happen to Listen to Roosevelt's Fireside Chat Tuesday Night (May 27)?

Economic Class	Yes	No
Upper	86%	14%
Middle	74	26
Lower	58	42

Source: OPOR Report, September 7, 1941, President's Secretary's Files.

TABLE 8
Would You Help England at the Risk of War to the United States?

	Yes
Upper income who listen	76%
Middle income who listen	71
Lower income who listen	67
Upper income who do not listen	63
Middle income who do not listen	58
Lower income who do not listen	53

Source: OPOR Report, September 7, 1941.

TABLE 9
Opinions Before and After Fireside Chat of December 29, 1940

	December 16	December 31	January 22
Which of these two things do you think more important for the United States to try to do:			
Keep out of war ourselves	39%	31%	36%
Help Britain even at the risk of getting into the war	57	66	59
No opinion	4	3	5

Source: OPOR Report, September 7, 1941.

levels after four weeks (see table 9). "Any increase in interventionist opinion resulting from a Presidential radio address," Cantril wrote in his report, "will not be maintained unless the address announces or is shortly followed by some action." [72]

After Pearl Harbor the content and tenor of public opinion reports submitted to the White House changed. Polling became less an academic exercise, more a tool in planning public information policy. [73] Trends were plotted on questions concerning America's war aims, attitudes towards allies, the persistence of isolationism and the adequacy of public information policy.

The initial public response to the Japanese attack, reported to Roosevelt by the Bureau of Intelligence, was one of unity behind the president and acceptance of his idealistic interpretation of America's role in the war. But this reflexive unity was superficial. Prewar isolationists continued to harbor anti-British and anti-Soviet sentiments, which were expressed in unflattering assessments of the war aims of America's allies. In a poll taken in early February 1942 and submitted to the White House in May, estimates of the war aims of the United States and its allies were elicited (table 10).

Anti-British views were interpreted as a reflection of the campaign waged by "a minority segment of the press led by the *New York Daily News* syndicate, *The Chicago Tribune* and the Hearst papers" to undermine Anglo-American unity. This campaign played on the clash between United States and British imperial interests, a theme that could be relied upon to evoke ancient prejudices. Remote parts of the British empire were not vital interests of the United States; Winston Churchill was an inadequate military commander and ally. Another theme was the failure of Great Britain to pay back its debts to the United States after World War I. This was the single most frequently invoked criticism among those unsympathetic to the alliance with Britain.

By March 1942 the Bureau of Intelligence reported that the wisdom of participation in a collective security organization and the error in not doing so after the first war were "self-evident" to most editorial writers, both Republican and Democrat. The bureau's polls showed that 85 percent now thought that the United States "should take an active part along with other nations in maintaining a world police force to guarantee against future wars." As recently as September 1939 the AIPO had asked: "Would you like to see the United States join in a movement to

TABLE 10

What Do You Think the United States (Russia, England) Is Really Fighting for in This War?

	United States	Soviet Union	England
An ideal	63%	15%	32%
Self-defense	21	49	31
Unsympathetic reasons	9	15	22
Miscellaneous reasons	3	—	1
Don't know	7	23	16
Total*	103	102	102

Source: Bureau of Intelligence Report, President's Secretary's Files, 170.
*Responses do not add up to 100% since the answers of some respondents were recorded in more than one category.

establish an international police force to maintain world peace?" Only 53 percent of those with opinions had said "yes."

In an access of optimism the bureau reported that isolationism was now a dead issue. It had become no more than a "misnomer to embrace pacifists, fascists, and persons whose enmity to the New Deal is so extreme as to set them in opposition to whatever it endorses." [74]

The premature nature of this judgment was clear before the end of 1942. Though isolationism as a response to attack was widely rejected, prewar isolationists did not renounce the views they had held before Pearl Harbor. In fact the numbers indicating that they had favored non-involvement before Pearl Harbor rose from 28 percent to 35 percent between November 1941 and July 1942. This finding led Cantril to predict that there would be no large-scale defection from the old isolationists in Congress. And indeed, the Congress that was returned in the midterm elections of 1942 contained strong enclaves of isolationism and anti-New Deal sentiment.

By the summer of 1943, the allegedly political tenor of OWI's home-front opinion and information work had become a critical problem in Elmer Davis's relations with Congress. Ironically, the more avowedly partisan opinion analysis emanating from Princeton escaped the attention of the president's congressional critics. Cantril prudently bypassed OWI in transmitting opinion data that dealt with partisan political strategy. Unlike the Bureau of Intelligence, Cantril's Princeton office was supported entirely from private funds and so was not subject to congressional scrutiny.

The role of opinion data in partisan political planning is well illustrated by exchanges between Princeton and the White House in March 1943. Cantril, himself a firm supporter of Roosevelt and the Democratic party, was looking ahead to the prospects for a fourth presidential term. Data gathered by Gallup and analyzed at Princeton were rather disquieting; support for FDR's candidacy among Democrats seemed to hinge on the state of the war. If peace were at hand it looked as though the president would lose quite a lot of ground. The troublesome figures are shown in table 11. Further analysis by party political preference revealed that almost the entire slippage was among Democrats.

David Niles, the presidential aid who at this time was Cantril's principal liaison at the White House, asked him whether this comparison could be kept out of print. Cantril cautioned against trying to influence Gallup in this way but offered the following words of encouragement: "Since this comparison and the cross-tabulations were made by me and since I have not heard Gallup or any of his people make the same observation, it seems to me likely that none of the Gallup outfit may see this point and you can be sure I will not draw attention to it." [75] In light of mounting

TABLE 11
Will You Vote for Roosevelt for a Fourth Term?

If the war is over and Roosevelt runs for a fourth term next year, do you think you will vote for him or against him?

For	37%
Against	50
No opinion	13

If the war is still going on and Roosevelt runs for a fourth term next year, do you think you will vote for him or against him?

For	53%
Against	36
No opinion	11

Source: "Notebooks of Cantril," vol. 2; the survey is dated February 23, 1943.

congressional complaints that war issues were being exploited to promote a fourth presidential term, it would not do for the opposition press
to perceive that the president's standing among his own constituents was
dependent on the continuation of hostilities. Cantril told Niles that it had
always been his policy to avoid influencing Gallup on decisions whether
to publish, "but I have tried to influence poll results by suggesting issues
and questions the vote on which I was fairly sure would be on the right
side." [76] Because of his good relations with Gallup, Cantril was in a
position to influence the questions tested in AIPO national surveys.

THE CONGRESSIONAL BACKLASH

It is fortunate that this correspondence remained stowed in the files at
Princeton and the White House. In the summer of 1943 congressional
attacks on the domestic activities of OWI reached a crescendo, and few
would have hesitated to assume guilt by association. But most opinion
reports were classified "confidential" or "restricted" so congressmen
were forced to concentrate their attacks on the more visible features of
OWI's operations. Of these the most vulnerable were its publications
and its budget.

In addition to the usual budget season charges of excess spending and
featherbedding, southern and Republican congressmen accused OWI of
involvement in "controversial" and "partisan" political issues. Gardner
Cowles, director of the domestic branch of OWI and an active Republican, had to counter the charge that publications of his organization were
"colored" with "New Dealism" in justifying his request for an appropriation of $8,865,906. [77] At the budget hearings on Capitol Hill Congress-
man Richard B. Wigglesworth of Massachusetts evoked shades of
Creel's congressional ordeal; he told OWI director Elmer Davis that
"considerable criticism" had come to his attention "on the general score
of the possible lack of loyalty in personnel now on the payrolls of the
agency." Davis was ominously reminded of his own membership in the
American Labor party. [78] Once again congressional immunity allowed
congressmen who could not pin down their frustration at partisan pleading to revert to generalized implications of disloyalty.

But these mild hints of congressional displeasure did not prevent the
House Appropriations Committee from recommending that $5.5 million
should be allocated to the domestic branch. This was a serious cut in

OWI funds and clearly required the curtailment of many of the organization's activities. Davis assessed the damage in a letter to Senator Kenneth McKeller, chairman of the Senate Appropriations Committee: "The reduction will require a drastic rearrangement of the domestic program particularly in the fields of publications, posters, motion pictures, special services and field operations." Any cut in these operations, Davis argued, would be a false economy since many would revert to other federal agencies and so would crop up again in other parts of the national budget. [79]

Despite the insinuations of disloyalty, the House committee's cuts represented a zeal for wartime economy as much as a politically motivated assault and were not fatal to the agency. However, when the national war agencies appropriation bill reached the floor of the House on June 18, OWI's domestic activities immediately came under more virulent attack. Congressman Joe Starnes of Alabama introduced an amendment that allocated $22.5 million to the overseas branch of OWI for propaganda and information work but *entirely* eliminated the appropriation for its domestic branch. It is worth pursuing the arguments used to justify this abrupt curtailment because they reflect many of the perennial tensions in legislative-executive relations, prompted by the government's shift into the information-public opinion field. These tensions, though apparent in an extreme form in the summer of 1943, also occurred during World War I and in a milder form in 1957 when they finally ended the State Department's own public-opinion polling.

Criticisms voiced by members of the House ranged from the specific to the most general. [80] They included the charge that OWI imposed its interpretation of American war aims (when the American people knew perfectly well why they were fighting); that it abridged the freedom of the press; that it harbored individuals of questionable loyalty (including the director); that its "New Dealism" was stirring up racial sentiment in the South and the big cities of the North; and, perhaps most seriously, that its information and public-opinion work acted as an advance guard preparing the ground for Roosevelt's reelection to a fourth term in 1944. Congressional hearings and debates revealed that this consideration was probably the decisive one.

The flavor of the assault on OWI's domestic work may be gained from the House debate. Starnes began by noting that the Appropriations Committee had already lopped $3 million or 37 percent off the funds for the domestic branch. This he took as an indication of general dissatisfaction with the branch's efficiency. But he thought the committee had not gone far enough: "The type and character of the domestic propaganda foisted on the American people through publications printed and distributed at government expense by the Office of War Information is a stench to the nostrils of a democratic people." [81] It was an insult to the patriotism of American congressmen and soldiers, Starnes continued, "to say that they do not know what they are fighting for until they are told what and why by the Office of War Information under the direction of Mr. Elmer Davis of the American Labor Party." OWI he charged, had "a distinct State socialist tinge." America "needs no Goebbels sitting in Washington to tell the American press what to publish or the American people why we are in the war, or to give a colored interpretation of any domestic program." Starnes confirmed that his amendment would "cut out all funds whatsoever" from the OWI for domestic use.

Other southern congressmen enlarged on Starnes's criticisms. Congressman John M. Robison of Kentucky pictured Davis, like President Roosevelt, using the funds supplied by Congress "to accomplish the ambitions of the President for a fourth term and continue the New Deal in power with its 3,008,000 office holders, and the policies, regulations and directives of these New Deal agencies and activities." Coming down firmly behind Starnes's amendment, he added:

> Believing that this $5,500,000 will be used for political purposes and to promote the fourth term of the President and a continuance of the bureaucratic control in Washington and the unwise policies of the New Deal, I am against this item in the appropriations bill and I hope it will be eliminated. [82]

Part of this complaint can be attributed to the eternal congressional frustration at the amount of "free publicity" that the president can generate thorough his prominence in the news. Such frustration naturally became more acute with a wartime presidential election impending. The president had every opportunity to appeal to the public as a national leader whose interests transcended petty legislative squabbling. Mrs. Eleanor Roosevelt had recently exacerbated the situation in a proposal made, presumably, with the president's approval. She suggested that all candidates for a particular public office be limited to equal campaign expenditures for advertising and travel. Expenditures were to be equalized and also paid for from public funds. This proposal appeared to many of the president's opponents as a ploy to reduce their visibility. It seemed particularly sinister when juxtaposed with the "tremendous influence" exercised over the radio, movies, and press by such Roosevelt partisans as Elmer Davis and Lowell Mellett, now director of the Bureau of Motion Pictures at OWI.

Although Mrs. Roosevelt's proposal confirmed these suspicions, the charges of partisanship and New Dealism were not new. In the previous section we noted that the Bureau of Intelligence linked lingering isolationism to distaste for anything, including in extreme cases the war effort, that smacked of the New Deal. The previous winter a minor political sensation had been caused by two OWI publications. The first was a glossy magazine *Victory*, prepared mainly for foreign distribution. Copies of the magazine had fallen into the hands of American servicemen, most of whom were on the electoral rolls. *Victory* carried a sketch of FDR and a story about vice-president Henry Wallace, parts of which Elmer Davis conceded were "indefensible." The offending profile of the president asserted that

Herbert Hoover was the candidate of "reactionaries" and the President defeated him because the country was "weary" of these. The New Deal was "just the program which could save the country from chaos" and was a huge success. The President so prepared the country for war that when it came he was ready to supply the anti-Axis nations quickly with what they needed. [83]

Victory also quoted Wallace's "Century of the Common Man" speech in which the American war effort and the bolshevik revolution were linked as part of the fight for the "people's revolution," whose first shots had been fired in the American War of Independence. It seemed particularly outrageous to the administration's opponents that $200,000 had already been spent on a publication that would boost the president's image at home and, through its "smugness and complacency," fail to win over legitimate target audiences abroad.

The second offensive publication to appear in the winter before the House decision to eliminate all funds for the domestic branch of OWI was a laudatory cartoon biography of President Roosevelt. It reminded Congressman John Taber of New York of the style used for the comic strip "Tarzan and the Apes." The congressman called the booklet "purely political propaganda, designed to promote a fourth term and a dictatorship."[84] It was of little avail for Davis to rejoin with the truism that it was common practice in wartime to exploit the head of government as a symbol of national unity. The relationship between the man in the White House and public opinion struck most of Roosevelt's critics as essentially a subnational or partisan issue, one that should not be cloaked in national symbolism.[85]

One of the problems OWI tackled both through surveys of opinion and publications was the position of black servicemen in the armed forces and their contribution to the war effort. A recent pamphlet, *Negroes and the War*, struck some southern congressmen as unconscionable executive meddling in problems that they were best equipped to handle themselves. Congressman Asa L. Allen of Louisiana chided Elmer Davis, "a member of the radical American Labor Party in New York," for spending the taxpayers' money on a pamphlet, running to 2.5 million copies, which, he said, undertook to "glorify one race in the war."

> We have a serious racial problem in this Nation. We in the South understand that problem and know best how to deal with it. We understand the psychology of the race problem . . . the type of propaganda which OWI has been sending out certainly does not hold that situation down.[86]

Writing in the *New York Times* Arthur Krock echoed congressional displeasure at the publication, but he was less concerned with its incendiary effect than with its partisanship. He quoted part of the pamphlet, with disapproval, representing it as an attempt to persuade blacks that they were beholden to the administration for any improvement in their position. It read in part:

> During the depression of the Thirties thousands of us [Negroes] were able to survive, even to make progress, because a friendly government through WPA and NRA, took a hand . . . . Since the advent of the New Deal the phrase "social security" has rung like a pleasant bell in the ears of American Negroes.[87]

For many conservative critics OWI's relations with the American public were altogether too colored by New Dealism, by radicals of questionable loyalty, by those who would abridge First Amendment rights, by advocates of war aims that sought to "globalize" the New Deal, by those who meddled in the racial problems of the South from the vantage point of New York and, most egregiously, by proponents of a fourth presidential term for Franklin Roosevelt. How much more virulent would the reaction have been if the House had been apprized of the content of the Princeton surveys considered in the previous section! Even without this additional kindling, the partisan character of the congressional reaction to domestic propaganda and public-opinion work was overwhelmingly apparant. It is revealed in the final House tally on the abolition of OWI's domestic operations (table 12). Democrats voting in favor of abolition were mostly southerners.

The House decision was greeted with surprise and anger from many quarters. To the director of OWI the decision spelled not only the curtailment of domestic operations but also an end to the whole information agency as originally conceived. The organization had been structured from the beginning to include two interdependent branches. This was partly for functional reasons and partly as a means of reconciling the different bureaucratic interests that had vied for the central position in the new superagency. Davis felt that its functioning would be fatally impaired if deprived of one of its two branches: "The Domestic Branch of the Office of War Information provides a number of *indispensable* services for the Overseas Branch. For example, the Domestic News Bureau gathers all governmental news in Washington—from Congress and from departments and agencies—for use in overseas broadcasts and new files." [88]

At a press conference the day after the House vote, Davis was especially bitter at the comparison that had been made with Goebbels on the House floor:

> I believe Representative Starnes of Alabama honored me by calling me the American Goebbels. There are quite a number of differ-

TABLE 12

Vote on War Agencies Appropriation Bill for Fiscal 1944, House of Representatives, June 18, 1943

	Democrats	Republicans	Others	Total
For abolition	55	160	3	128
Against abolition	108	5	1	114

ences as Mr. Starnes could discover by reading the record. The only difference I would like to point out is that Dr. Goebbels does not have to go to the Reichstag for his appropriation. We think we have been doing a job worth doing and at less expense than it could be done in any other way. It would obviously cost a great deal more to have each government agency in Washington doing the job on its own.[89]

Many of the organs of opinion whose independence had allegedly been infringed by his agency sided with Davis. In fact considerable pressure built up to have the Senate reinstate the domestic branch of OWI. This pressure came not only from northern, Democratic, and liberal sources but also from editors, press associations, and radio stations in southern and border states. The point-by-point rebuttals offered by these sources is indicative of the gap between congressional and editorial opinion.

The *Louisville* (Kentucky) *Courier-Journal* took Congressman Allen to task for his misrepresentation of the pamphlet *Negroes and the War*. Far from inciting race prejudice in the South, the pamphlet, "addressed to Negro workers, was an appeal to them to take pride in their efforts, to take glory in their opportunity to serve their Nation in its extremity." It was incomprehensible to the editors of the *Courier-Journal* that "even the most expeditious panderer to inflammable prejudice should cavil at such a word of encouragement for Americans working to help save America."[90] Modern sensibilities might be aroused by the implication of privilege on the part of black servicemen for being permitted to suffer casualties out of proportion to their number. But in the 1943 context, the *Courier-Journal*'s editorial amounted to a brave stand against "wanton irresponsibility" and prejudice.[91]

In the Senate hearings, Senator Gerald Nye returned to the pamphlet and reported that he had received many anonymous communications attributing part of the recent ferment in Detroit to its circulation there. Senator Henry Cabot Lodge condemned its praise of social security as a boon to the Negro for which the New Deal was to be thanked.

These complaints went a little too far even for the Republican press. The *New York Herald Tribune* retorted that the congressmen had failed to grasp (or were willfully ignoring) the counterpropaganda elements in the pamphlet.[92] Even in World War I the Germans had appealed to all ethnic groups with a grievance against the Allies.[93] *Negroes and the War* was directed against enemy propaganda, known to be circulating in New York City, Chicago, and Detroit, that the Negro was in such dire straits in America that he had nothing to lose from defeat and no personal interest in American victory. Cantril's surveys repeatedly showed that the lower socioeconomic groups felt that they would be less affected personally by a German victory. The pamphlet's introduction quoted from *Mein Kampf* to show what the Negroes could expect from the Nazis: "It is a criminal absurdity," Hitler wrote, "to train a born half-ape until one believes a lawyer had been made of him . . . for it is training exactly as that of a poodle." It then went on to demonstrate how contrary Hitler's defamations were to the policy of the government of the United States, citing as evidence the progress of blacks in the professions and social security. The pamphlet then asked, "What kind of social security could they [Negro youth] expect under Nazi rule?"[94] This debate was defused, in any event, by the new domestic director Palmer Hoyt (like his predecessor a Republican) who announced that he intended to discontinue all domestic publications except the most functional regulations.

Other sources in the mass media ridiculed the insinuations of disloyalty that had been hurled at OWI and its top administrators. Picking up Starnes's references to Mr. Davis's membership, or former membership, in the American Labor party one radio commentator noted: "Many folks would say that was no more sin than being a Democrat or Republican."[95] With just a touch of hyperbole a CBS commentator reminded his listeners that "the domestic bureau of War Information was set up and operated by rockribbed Republicans."[96]

Nor did Starnes's complacent assumption that the American people were sufficiently well informed about the war aims of the United Nations go unchallenged. Foreshadowing Kriesberg's discovery of "dark areas of ignorance" the *Chattanooga Times* found "a good basis for the belief that the American people and especially many members of Congress do indeed need to be 'sold' on the war."[97] This need arose not only from the vestiges of isolationism but also, and more simply, from the fact that "a great many people are pretty fuzzy about the war aims."[98] "It's a sad fact," Claude Mahoney observed, "that both the Army and the Navy find it necessary to have heavy classes on just that subject."[99] By comparison with the British and the Russians, let alone the Nazis, the Americans were doing little enough to clarify the stakes involved in the war even for the men at the front. It is perhaps testimony to the success of the system of self-censorship that no commentators attributed public confusion about America's political war aims to Roosevelt's tendency to delay their precise formulation.

Another pretext for the abolition of the domestic branch of OWI was its alleged interference with First Amendment rights. OWI's news bureau was said to have abridged the freedom of the press in exercising its powers of clearance and coordination. It was one of the bureau's jobs to rewrite stories emanating from other government departments.

This particular complaint was surprising. First, the powers of censorship had been lodged in a separate office. In this OWI differed from the Creel committee in World War I. Second, the profession that Starnes cast in the role of victim showed little awareness of its own predicament. On the contrary, important members of the journalistic profession, not known for its submissiveness, expressed their willingness to continue to cooperate with OWI.

Congressman Emanuel Cellar of New York inserted into the *Congressional Record* communications from various professional editorial associations approving the activities of the news bureau. While scarcely eulogizing OWI, many of these communications indicated that the press considered the organization invaluable. It was obviously far more convenient for reporters to extract their news about government operations from a central bureau than to go the rounds from one bureaucracy to another. They did not feel that their freedom of enquiry into matters neglected by the OWI "filter" was thereby abridged.

Several of these letters took the form of petitions to the Senate Appropriations Committee to revoke the action of the House. A single example will suffice. Milton Murray, president of the American Newspaper Guild, wrote: "On behalf of the members of the American Newspaper Guild, I request that full appropriations be voted for adequate operation of the Domestic Branch of the Office of War Information, at least to the extent proposed by the Budget Bureau." [100] Murray's confidence is particularly striking when it is considered that four days before the House vote, Davis had made a controversial speech before the guild's convention in Boston. He criticized those "gentlemen [of the press] who do not take the trouble to check up on the accuracy of what they write." [101] Davis's remarks made their way to the floor of the Senate extremely rapidly. The following day Senator Styles Bridges of New Hampshire told his colleagues:

I cannot and shall not stand idly by while our American press is openly scored by a man who has sought to create the first United States Government propaganda bureau of a kind used in the dictator countries. [Mr. Davis is seeking] to silence the Nation's press to cover sins of maladministration on the part of the New Deal in the war effort. [102]

Predictably, Senator Bridges found time to refer to Davis's background as "chairman of the radical American Labor Party in New York." Congressional opponents of the administration, like Senator Styles, succeeded in outdistancing the press in their zeal for the prerogatives of the fourth branch.

It was against this background that Elmer Davis and Milton Eisenhower attempted to persuade the Senate Appropriations Committee to restore the funds the House eliminated. Davis appealed to the economy-minded senators by pointing out that most of the cuts would simply create a balloon effect, because the items would reappear in the budgets of a plethora of other agencies. Not only would these informational activities be more expensive if dispersed throughout the bureaucracy, they would also be less efficient.

Senator Rufus C. Holman, who had previously read the offending publication *Victory* into the *Congressional Record*, took up the charge of political propaganda, asserting that such publications would have a "great political effect" in United States politics through the medium of American servicemen. Davis rejoined by drawing the senators' attention to the variegated political sentiments of his staff, many of whom were staunch Republicans: "If I were going to try to build up an organization for partisan propaganda, I think I would have sense enough not to build it so that half of it could always neutralize the other half." [103]

The senators' strictures that OWI keep away from controversial issues could be followed, Davis said, only if some definition of "controversial" were provided. In the absence of such a definition, the agency attempted to state both sides of any issue. This was particularly the case with presidential candidates. Since either man might become president of the United States, OWI felt the need to "build up" both of them. This was being done with Willkie and Governor Dewey as well as FDR. [104]

Professional advertisers, like Paul B. West, president of the Association of National Advertisers, and Chester J. LaRoche, chairman of the

War Advertising Council, also testified in favor of restoring the funds, but they did not always present their case felicitously. LaRoche's argument that OWI played a vital part in "guiding and directing" popular opinion awoke senatorial suspicions of a direct executive line to vox populi. "In all this guiding and directing peoples' thought," Senator Holman mused, "it is amazing to me that they have any independent thoughts left." [105] LaRoche rejoined that information work did no more than harness well-tired advertising techniques to the national interest.

As a result of these hearings the Senate subcommittee voted to restore part of OWI's domestic funding. It recommended the sum of $3,561,499, considerably less than the $5,500,000 first proposed by the House committee but a reprieve from the total elimination voted on the House floor. When the bill reached the floor of the Senate it was clear that both the House's immolation and the senate committee's surgery were really bargaining positions from which both sides were prepared to negotiate. The curtailment was, in all probability, voted by the House in the knowledge that the Senate would restore part of the funding. In this way, opposition congressmen could vent their displeasure, reduce the intensity of OWI's relations with the public, and yet avoid the opprobrium of hampering an important part of the home front war effort. The Senate agreed to cut a further $811,499 from the appropriation and House conferees accepted the figure of $2,750,000, scarcely more than a quarter of Cowles's original request. [106]

Despite the brave face put on the situation by Davis and Hoyt, congressional action meant the eclipse of OWI as the principal link between the government and the public on wartime and postwar issues. The extent of its eclipse can be judged by the drop in funds from $8.8 million in 1943 to $2.7 million in 1944. As the congressional scene darkened Davis predicted that even a cut back to $3.0 million would mean that "about two thirds of the work of the Domestic Branch will have to be liquidated and more than half our personnel will have to be released." [107]

The situation in early July was even more serious than this. Under Hoyt's reorganization the personnel was reduced from 1,269 to 491 and many operations were eliminated. [108] Hoyt's directorship, coinciding with the budget cuts, inaugurated a period when the domestic branch would abandon any role in domestic propaganda or policy decision making and confine its activities to the facilitation of the flow of war news to the press.

World War II precipitated an intensification of the opinion-policy relationship. Once an unlimited national emergency was recognized steps were taken to control the flow of information to the public, and regular procedures were inaugurated for the submission of opinion to the executive. Two channels were established for the submission of opinion, one formal and one informal. The formal channel was the Bureau of Intelligence of OFF and then OWI. It analyzed themes of topical importance in public opinion and transmitted its findings to policy makers in intelligence reports. The informal channel was provided by the Office of Public Opinion Research at Princeton, whose findings were transmitted to the White House by Hadley Cantril.

OWI also became the key intermediary for the diffusion of information to the public. Its campaigns and publications were designed to awaken enthusiasm for the war effort, to increase understanding of American war aims, to encourage friendship for America's allies, and to lay the foundations for public acceptance of a postwar order based on collective security. Its campaigns were designed to fill those areas of ignorance revealed by Bureau of Intelligence surveys.

OWI failed to achieve that "management of opinion" which Harold Lasswell wrote, in 1927, was "an unescapable corollary of modern war." Its failure can be attributed to several factors. First, existing parts of the bureaucracy felt their "essential missions" and "autonomy" to be threatened. Elmer Davis was an insufficiently experienced bureaucratic player to assert the prerogatives of his organization early enough. It therefore lost the opportunity to obtain equal standing, and an equal probability of being consulted, with existing organizations. For an agency whose information dealt with foreign affairs, poor relations with the State Department were a disaster.

Second, the organization seemed to encroach on the domain of Congress. It did not treat Congress as the voice of popular opinion but, in accordance with its mandate from the president, sought to establish a direct relationship with the public. This relationship seemed to many congressmen too suffused with New Deal sentiment. They accused the organization of partisan pleading and fatally weakened its domestic operations in the summer of 1943.

Because the director of OWI failed to establish his right to be consulted he never became an indispensable submitter of opinion. Informal channels were always more important and remained so after the debilitation of OWI. As we shall see these informal channels were supplemented, between 1943 and 1947, by the Office of Public Affairs in the State Department. This office utilized many of the techniques and personnel that had failed to reach full effectiveness in OWI. In this way OWI and the continuing operations of Hadley Cantril provided a bridge between the prewar and the postwar opinion-policy relationship.

NOTES

1. Harold Lasswell, *Propaganda Technique in World War I* (Cambridge, Mass., 1971), p. 15. Originally published as *Propaganda Technique in the World War* (London, 1927).
2. The system of censorship was largely voluntary but the Committee on Public Information could invoke the 1917 Espionage Act and ask the Justice Department to prosecute. The act could also be used as the basis for seizing films on the ground that they were likely to promote the success of America's enemies. See Title 1, Section 3, Espionage Act, 1917.
3. James J. Best, *Public Opinion, Micro and Macro* (Homewood, Ill., 1973), p. 222.
4. Morton H. Halperin and Arnold Kanter, *Readings in American Foreign Policy: A Bureaucratic Perspective* (Boston, 1973), pp. 10-11.
5. Lasswell, *Propaganda Technique*, p. 37.
6. For discussion of the player analogy, see Halperin and Kanter, *Readings*, p. 9.
7. For an account of the orientation toward public opinion of the two presidents that stresses dispositional factors, see Manfred Landecker, *The President and Public Opinion: Leadership in Foreign Affairs* (Washington, D.C., 1968).
8. Alexander George and Juliet George, *Woodrow Wilson and Colonel House: A Personality Study* (New York, 1956).
9. Interview with John Sloan Dickey, former director of the Office of Public Affairs, Department of State, in Hanover, New Hampshire, on April 17, 1973. For a discussion of the stratification of public opinion see chapter 7.
10. Lansing, Baker, and Daniels to Wilson, April 12, 1917, cited by James R. Mock and Cedric Larson, *Words That Won the War: The Story of the Committee on Public Information, 1917-1919* (Princeton, 1939), p. 51.
11. Unpublished study prepared for the OWI, National Archives, "Office of War Information" Files, Record Group 208, Box 64 (referred to hereafter as "OWI Study").
12. The committee's structure went through several changes. For details see George Creel, *Complete Report of the Chairman of the Committee on Public Information* (Washington D.C., 1920), and George Creel, *How We Advertised America* (New York, 1920).
13. Senator Boies Penrose from Pennsylvania, cited by Lasswell, *Propaganda Technique*, p. 45.
14. Ibid., p. 29.
15. "A British member of Parliament," Lasswell recalls," once called attention to a laudatory illustrated biography of the Prime Minister (Lloyd George) which was being circulated at public expense as part of British war propaganda." Ibid., p. 39.

16. "OWI Study."
17. See T. Swann Harding, "Information Techniques of the Department of Agriculture," *Public Opinion Quarterly* (Winter 1936-1937).
18. Cited by T. Swann Harding, "Genesis of One 'Government Propaganda Mill,'" *Public Opinion Quarterly* (Summer 1947).
19. For the notion of introversion in foreign policy, see Lloyd A. Free, "The Introversion-Extroversion Cycle in National Mood in Recent Decades" (Paper prepared for the Annual Conference of the American Association for Public Opinion Research, Asheville, North Carolina, May 18, 1973).
20. See John Stoessinger, *Nations in Darkness* (New York, 1971).
21. Peter G. Filene, *Americans and the Soviet Experiment, 1917-1933: American Attitudes towards Russia from the February Revolution until Diplomatic Recognition* (Cambridge, Mass., 1967).
22. See Chapter 1 for a discussion of the stages of the decision process.
23. One occasion when Hull did stir himself to fight extreme isolationist pressure was in opposing the Ludlow resolution after the sinking of the U.S.S. *Panay* by the Japanese in December 1937. The law, which was narrowly defeated in the House, would have made a referendum mandatory before the United States could declare war. Cordell Hull, *The Memoirs of Cordell Hull* (New York, 1948), pp. 563-564.
24. John Sloan Dickey, "The Secretary and the American Public," in Don K. Price, ed., *The Secretary of State* (Englewood Cliffs, 1960), p. 144.
25. "Trade Agreements," n.d., Cordell Hull Papers, Box 89, Library of Congress.
26. "Trade Agreements, 1933-1935," Hull Papers, Box 89.
27. Dickey, "Secretary and the American Public," p. 144.
28. Dickey interview.
29. Dickey, "Secretary and the American Public," p. 144.
30. "Foreign Policy—General," Hull Papers, Box 65.
31. "OWI Study."
32. The phrase is Roosevelt's. See Gloria Barron, *Leadership in Crisis* (New York, 1973), p. 47.
33. Executive Order 8248, *Code of Federal Regulations, 1938-1943, Title 3—The President*, Compilation (Washington, D.C., 1968), p. 578. The establishment of OGR was part of President Roosevelt's Reorganization Plan II.
34. Lowell Mellett, "Government Propaganda," *The Atlantic Monthly* (September 1941). The reference was probably to Archibald MacLeish or Harold Ickes. Ickes, in particular, was exasperated by Mellett's seeming complacency about the condition of public opinion in face of the world crisis.
35. Roosevelt to O'Leary, February 1941, cited by Margaret Hicks Williams, "'The President's' Office of Government Reports," *Public Opinion Quarterly* (Winter 1941).
36. Mellett, "Government Propaganda," p. 311.
37. Ibid., p. 312.
38. Cited by Landecker, *President and Public Opinion*, p. 26.
39. "OWI Study."
40. Ibid. Emphasis added.
41. Ibid.
42. *The Secret Diary of Harold L. Ickes, III* (New York, 1954), p. 426.

43. Unpublished study of the predecessors of the Office of Facts and Figures by Harold F. Gosnell, dated September 23, 1943. Archibald MacLeish Papers, Box 37, Library of Congress (referred to hereafter as "OFF Study").

44. MacLeish to Harold D. Smith, director, Budget Bureau, October 22, 1941, MacLeish Papers, Box 37.

45. MacLeish to Hopkins, October 27, 1941, Harry Hopkins Papers, File 324, Franklin D. Roosevelt Library, Hyde Park.

46. For a more general discussion of OFF, see R. K. Kane, "The OFF," *Public Opinion Quarterly* (Summer 1942).

47. "OFF Study."

48. Release, Archibald MacLeish, then Librarian of Congress, October 21, 1941, MacLeish Papers, Box 37.

49. *New York Times*, February 15, 1942.

50. "The Wartime Notebooks of Hadley Cantril." The six notebooks are available, with special permission, from the Roper Center, Williams College. Most of the pages are not numbered.

51. Jerome E. Edwards, *The Foreign Policy of Colonel McCormick's Tribune* (Reno, Nevada, 1971), contains much useful information on the paper's editorial line.

52. MacLeish to Harold D. Smith, director, Budget Bureau, February 20, 1942, cited by "OFF Study."

53. "OWI Study."

54. *New York Times*, April 4, 1942.

55. Cited by "OFF Study."

56. See, for example, Richard Neustadt's discussion of the Skybolt decision in *Alliance Politics* (New York 1970).

57. Roger Burlingame, *Don't Let Them Scare You: The Life and Times of Elmer Davis* (Philadelphia, 1961).

58. Cedric Larson, "The British Ministry of Information," *Public Opinion Quarterly* (Fall 1941).

59. "Report to the President, 1942-1945," Elmer Davis Papers, OWI Subject File, Box 10, Library of Congress.

60. Roosevelt to Hull, September 1, 1943, National Archives, OWI Files, Record Group 208. Federal Records Center, Suitland, Maryland.

61. Lasswell, *Propaganda Technique*, p. 28.

62. "OWI Study."

63. "Cantril Notebooks," vol. 1. Cantril to Rosenberg, September 1, 1942.

64. Cantril to Roosevelt, March 7, 1941, Official File, No. 857, Roosevelt Library.

65. Later in the war Cantril wrote to Grace Tully: "In view of the forecast of another meeting of the big three [Yalta], I thought some of our recent information on public understanding of and opinion toward Russia might be of interest to the President." Cantril to Tully, November 10, 1944, President's Secretary's File, No. 173, Roosevelt Library. Evidently the White House did not share Cantril's sense of urgency about the bearing of the data on the coming negotiations for Grace Tully attached the following note to Cantril's letter: "Nice letter thanking Mr. Cantril. The President was much interested in reading it [latest report] and hopes to see him one of these days soon." Initialed CGT with the additional comment, "Give General Watson to arrange an appointment sometime—no hurry."

66. President's Secretary's Files, No. 173.
67. Department of State, *Peace and War, United States Foreign Policy, 1931-1941* (Washington, D.C., 1943).
68. Cited by Robert A. Divine, *Roosevelt and World War II* (Baltimore, 1969), p. 43.
69. James MacGregor Burns, *Roosevelt: The Soldier of Freedom* (New York, 1970), pp. 92-93.
70. Report, Cantril to the White House, July 3, 1941, President's Secretary's Files, No. 173.
71. "Comparison of Opinions of Those Who Do and Do Not Listen to the President's Radio Talks," confidential report submitted to the White House, September 1941, President's Secretary's Files, No. 170.
72. Ibid. The causal implications of these surveys were weak. The president's radio audience may have been disproportionately composed of those predisposed in favor of intervention.
73. Confidential Report submitted to the White House by the Bureau of Information entitled "Americans and the War," undated. FDRL, PSF, 173.
74. Ibid.
75. Cantril to Niles, March 23, 1943, "Cantril Notebooks," vol. 2.
76. Ibid.
77. House, Subcommittee of the Committee on Appropriations, *Hearings on the National War Agencies Appropriations Bill for 1944*, 78th Cong., 1st sess., 1943, pp. 984-985.
78. Ibid., p. 1055.
79. Davis to McKeller, June 18, 1943. Senate, Subcommittee of the Committee on Appropriations, *Hearings on H.R. 2968*, 78th Cong., 1st sess., 1943, p. 174.
80. *Congressional Record*, June 18, 1943, pp. 6132-6133.
81. Ibid., pp. 6133-6134.
82. Ibid., p. 6136.
83. *New York Times*, February 14, 1943.
84. Ibid., March 5, 1943.
85. Lloyd George met similar criticism from the House of Commons in World War I when it was discovered that an illustrated biography of the prime minister was being distributed to rally public morale.
86. *Congressional Record*, June 18, 1943, p. 6136.
87. *New York Times*, July 8, 1943.
88. Davis to McKeller, June 19, 1943, in Senate, *Hearings, on H.R. 2968*, p. 178.
89. *New York Times*, June 20, 1943.
90. *Louisville* (Kentucky) *Courier-Journal*, June 20, 1943.
91. *The Atlanta* (Georgia) *Constitution*, June 22, 1943, pointed out that racial tensions were a national problem due not to the machinations of OWI but to "overcrowded cities, overcrowded working areas, overcrowded transportation lines, lack of housing, lack of recreation."
92. *New York Herald Tribune*, February 7, 1943. The story predated the House action but was read into the *Congressional Record* by Mr. Cellar of New York after the vote for abolition.
93. Lasswell, *Propaganda Technique*, p. 151.
94. Senate, *Hearings on H.R. 2968*, p. 197.

95. Claude Mahoney, June 19, 1943. Appendix to the *Congressional Record*, 89, II pp. A3308-A3311.
96. Jay Franklin, June 23, 1943. For these and other radio commentaries cited see the appendix to the *Congressional Record* 89, pt. II, pp. A3308-A3311.
97. *Chattanooga Times*, June 20, 1943.
98. Mahoney, *Congressional Record*.
99. Ibid.
100. Murray to Kenneth McKellar, chairman, Senate Appropriations Committee. See *Appendix to the Congressional Record*, 89, pt. II, p. A3312. Similar messages were inserted into the record from other representatives of the profession.
101. *New York Times*, June 15, 1943.
102. Ibid., June 16, 1943.
103. Senate, *Hearings on H.R. 2968*, p. 186.
104. *New York Times*, July 8, 1943.
105. Senate, *Hearings on H.R. 2968*, p. 265.
106. See *New York Times*, July 2, 6, 1943; *Congressional Record* 89, pt. 5, pp. 6800-6828.
107. Davis to McKeller, June 29, 1943, in Senate, *Hearings on H.R. 2968*, p. 406.
108. *New York Times*, August 15, 1943.

4

Public opinion comes of age

THE STATE DEPARTMENT REGAINS THE INITIATIVE

One of the effects of World War II was to intensify the relationship between American policy makers and the public. Popular opinion was regularly canvassed and the results transmitted to the president and cabinet officers. There were several channels for the submission of opinion data: OWI, private survey organizations (such as OPOR at Princeton), and the public information bureaus of various federal departments. The diffusion of information to the public also reached a new height of intensity with campaigns to mobilize opinion on many war-related themes.

Despite the intensity, this activity was far less successful than its principal exponents hoped. In part this was because of the president's preference for informal channels and his reluctance to continue to provide the backing needed if these new organizations were to gain bureaucratic ascendancy. In part, too, it suffered from the jealously of the Congress, which feared that its own role as spokesman for public opinion was being challenged. Although the New Deal strengthened the presidency immeasurably, only the war propelled the executive into an equally dominant position in foreign affairs. Legislative anger at this apparent usurpation often fixed on those agents of the president's will whom the war had thrust into prominent, and hence exposed, positions. Ultimately the expression of this anger redounded not to the advantage of the Congress itself but to that of older line departments that had been overshadowed by the bureaucratic creatures of war.

OWI's domestic branch was a victim of these dynamics and of its own inexperience and ineptitude in the bureaucratic game. OWI officers took the view that the cutback Congress ordered in the summer of 1943 stemmed from legislative-executive tensions, exacerbated by partisan suspicions. Milton Eisenhower, whose report lay behind the establishment of OWI in the first place, gave his postmortem to Stephen Early, the president's press secretary: "We took a beating on the domestic end of things, not because we were doing a poor job, but because the Congress was trying to discredit an agency which it felt might work too enthusiastically for the President."[1] But even with the drastic loss of funds and curtailment of domestic activities, the acting director of OWI hoped that something could still be salvaged. "The fundamental necessity now," he told Early, "is for the President to do something appropriate to restore the prestige of OWI." And, indeed, the president did issue directives urging other departments engaged in war work to cooperate more closely with the vestigial OWI. On September 1, 1943, a month after Eisenhower communicated with Early, Roosevelt wrote to the secretary of state urging "a closer relationship between the Department of State and the Office of War Information."[2]

This had little effect, and OWI officials continued to be frustrated by their exclusion from significant policy discussions and by their difficulty in even obtaining information from the State Department about its decisions. In late October Elmer Davis and Robert Sherwood, the overseas director of OWI, told Stettinius, who had just been named under secretary of state, that "they did not feel things were going smoothly between OWI and the Department."[3] They had even heard that the State Department was keeping a dossier of "OWI sins." But Stettinius's reassurances scarcely disguised the fact that the initiative had passed out of OWI's hands.

In part this was because the war itself had entered a new "political" phase. After the German defeat at Stalingrad the previous winter it appeared increasingly unlikely that the Axis would be able to resume its great offensives of 1941 and 1942.[4] Victory was by no means assured, yet the collapse of Italy and the failure of Hitler's Russian campaign boded well for the Allies. This made postwar planning imperative. Such planning was the forte not of ad hoc wartime agencies like OWI but of political experts in the White House and State Department. State Department planners rapidly came to the conclusion that negotiations with the Allies and the mobilization of public support for the victors' peace were interdependent. Wilson's failure to grasp this point was widely assumed to have led to America's self-exclusion from the League of Nations in 1919. To avoid a repetition of this disaster the department plunged into public-opinion work. Through a series of administrative reforms and high-level personnel changes the department soon established itself as the principal intermediary between policy makers and the public. Sporadic collaboration with OWI continued until that organization's final liquidation in September 1945; but there was little doubt about the identity of its senior partner. As a sign of the times most of Hadley Cantril's reports were rerouted from the Bureau of Intelligence, OWI, to the Office of the Special Consultant at State, and Cantril himself became a State Department consultant.

Postwar planning elevated the Department of State to a critical position in the opinion-policy relationship. The task of educating the American public to the responsibilities of collective security and world leadership provided the department with a vehicle both to shape postwar institutions and to refurbish its own image. This happy coincidence of interests stimulated two administrative reorganizations of the department and the creation of new machinery specifically charged with public affairs. Its methods and personnel drew on the obsolescent domestic branch of OWI. Its information campaigns interwove the themes of collective security, the democratic formulation of foreign policy, and the vital functions the Department of State performed. After the "multimedia" campaign that led up to the San Francisco conference, the public could, perhaps, be forgiven for reaching the conclusion that the success of the United Nations and the success of the State Department in penetrating the living rooms of America were one and the same. In a pretelevision age, foreign policy leaders made a unique debut in the media of popular communications and entertainment.

The relative eclipse of the State Department in fashioning the country's foreign policy and in relating that policy to public opinion can be traced to three factors. First, during his long tenure as secretary of state, Cordell Hull was preoccupied with foreign economic policy; in the 1930s he was unwilling to challenge the isolationist phalanx in Congress. Issues of high policy eluded the department, being the prerogatives of the legislature and, to an increasing extent, of the White House.[5] The periodic renewals of the trade agreements were the only occasions for the department's conspicuous entrance into the public arena during the period, and even then its targets were confined to the opinion elite, particularly congressmen.

Second, the department operated in war under the shadow of a network of emergency agencies. These included the joint chiefs of staff, established after Pearl Harbor to facilitate coordination with the British; the Office of Lend-Lease Administration; the War Resources Board; the Office of Strategic Services; the Office of Emergency Management; the Inter-American Defense Board; the Office of War Information; and countless others. In addition, other old line agencies became more deeply embroiled in foreign affairs. "New foreign policy bureaucracies responsible to other, more powerful agencies, came increasingly to overshadow the State Department. At the height of the war, forty-four separate government agencies had representatives stationed at the American embassy in London."[6]

The third factor tending to diminish the department's influence was the style of Roosevelt's foreign-policy leadership. Thomas M. Campbell's reappraisal of Hull's influence is only partially correct: "It is a myth," he writes, "that during the war Roosevelt was his own Secretary of State."[7] As evidence Campbell refers to Hull's energetic pursuit of collective security and his plan "to remold the world along lines that would aggrandize the national economy and spread democratic ideology." True, Hull had lost none of his free trading fervor, although it is not clear that this amounted to a program for national aggrandizement. But his involvement in high policy was largely limited to the U.N. project, which flourished during the last year of his eleven-year incumbency. Otherwise he endured under Secretary Sumner Welles's preeminence in policy planning and White House liaison until September 1943. At that time the president, considering a fourth term and deferring to Hull's domestic political influence, finally agreed to exact Welles's resignation.[8]

Even then, the president was far more likely to consult Harry Hopkins or Admiral Leahy than State Department officers. Diplomatic channels of communication went into partial disuse in favor of army and navy channels. The president had immediate access to these through the map room, which he had established in the White House. If the secretary of state saw these cables or policy memorandums at all, he was usually required to return them to the White House without keeping a copy.[9] It is clear from this that one of the State Department's objectives during its "revitalization" campaign was to enhance its reputation with the president and not just with the public and the Congress. This would increase the department's probability of being consulted, one of the criteria of bureaucratic effectiveness suggested by Halperin and Kanter.[10]

These three factors, then, contributed to the State Department's difficulties. Hull was not spared criticism from his contemporaries. Leading Congressmen were dissatisfied with their State Department liaison. Press complaints about political ineffectiveness were, to some extent, met by the more political phase of the war which brought the department into postwar planning.[11] Hull's performance at the meeting of foreign ministers in Moscow in October 1943 won a positive response even from former critics. The advent of Stettinius brought two drastic reorganizations (the first had been planned by Hull), which helped to improve the department's image.

Edward Stettinius took office as under secretary of state on October 4, 1943, replacing Sumner Welles. He served in this capacity, much of the time as acting secretary because of Hull's absence abroad and illness, until November 1944 when he became secretary of state. He remained in this position for seven months until June 27, 1945, when President Truman accepted his resignation.

Scarcely an expert on foreign affairs, Stettinius owed his appointment to his acceptability to both Hull and Roosevelt and to his reputation as a sound administrator and good public-relations man, talents he had acquired in business as a phenomenally young chairman of U.S. Steel and in government at the War Resources Board and the Lend-Lease Administration.[12] He was a personal friend of Harry Hopkins and worked with him on lend-lease. His tenure at State coincided with major reorientation in American foreign policy whose groundwork had been laid by a special postwar research group, which began meeting at State under the chairmanship of Leo Pasvolsky in 1942. These deliberations culminated in the draft Four Nations Declaration, which Hull took with him to Moscow in October 1943 when Stettinius first became acting secretary. The draft contained a firm commitment to American participation in the proposed internaitonal security organization.

Stettinius's appointment also coincided with the low point in the department's standing with the public. Special consultant John Sloan

Dickey confided to a colleague one month after the new under secretary's arrival that "the point has been reached where there can be no question concerning the widespread dissatisfaction and doubt which exists in all circles regarding the State Department as an institution."[13] The reorganization that Stettinius introduced in January 1944 was designed to cut through this malaise. It affected the entire department but "the changes in the functions and organization relating to popular education were one of the most conspicuous features."[14] Stettinius displayed the same zeal in the campaign to revitalize the department's image as he did in his efforts to mobilize support for the United Nations. Public opinion assumed a rare prominence in department policy making under Stettinius.

Hull was appalled at the little attention the public paid to the great issues of state and at its fascination with news of a "temporary or trivial nature." It became part of the department's conventional wisdom in 1944 that "an informed public opinion relating to basic international questions" was indispensable to American foreign policy. As the secretary told his news conference on July 11: "There has never been greater need for an alert public opinion than there is today. It will continue to be increasingly greater until victory has crowned our efforts and post-war problems have been settled."[15]

As a first step toward meeting this need, Hull had appointed a special consultant in June 1943 to monitor the department's relations with the public. The appointment of John Sloan Dickey to this position represented the first attempt to generalize the experience in information work gained during the periodic renewals of the trade agreements. But, as in the economic sphere, the target stratum of the public for the special consultant's activities was limited to the policy and opinion elite. No effort was made to reach the attentive or mass public. The implicit model of the opinion-policy relationship was one in which organized groups of the public, often constituted as lobbies, would be persuaded of the wisdom of the government's position in order that they, in turn, might influence members of Congress.[16] But the far-reaching implications of the Four Nations Declaration from Moscow seemed to demand a more ambitious information program since it presaged a major reorientation in America's place in world politics. The State Department's need to reach a wider public also arose from OWI's virtual exclusion from this work by congressional action in the summer of 1943.

Accordingly, the reorganization of January 1944 set up an Office of Public Information under Dickey's direction. It was in charge of relations with private groups and organizations interested in the formulation of foreign policy; collection and analysis of public attitude data; research on international affairs; and the publication of official documents. Its operating divisions recalled, to some extent, the structure of the domestic branch of OWI. [17] The departmental order of January 15 gave Dickey a mandate to carry opinion and information work beyond the confines of organized interest groups to the general public. It set up machinery for the weekly and fortnightly surveys of opinion that the department conducted in succeeding years.

Dickey's office was accorded a position equivalent to that of the major regional and specialized offices, such as the Office of Far Eastern Affairs or Economic Affairs. But the new structure did not seem to accord public opinion specialists the *policy* role that Pasvolsky had called for. Admittedly Dickey was, ex officio, a member of the two major policy committees in the department. Opinion analysis conducted under his direction did reach policy officials and major foreign outposts during 1944. But, at the assistant secretary level, public opinion was handled by Howland Shaw, who was also responsible for general and foreign service administration. After some notable failures in the dissemination of information on postwar planning [18] pressure built up for representation of public-opinion work by an officer high enough in the department to wield some authority.

Departmental order 1301 of December 17, 1944, which provided for an assistant secretary of state for public and cultural relations, gave public opinion and information work what Dickey called "organizational parity" within the department. [19] Archibald MacLeish was the main candidate for this position. At the same time Pasvolsky gained the equivalent rank of an assistant secretary with the title special assistant to the secretary in charge of international organization and security. [20] The simultaneous elevation of public affairs and international organization was significant: "It was the U.N. project which brought the public affairs function to full flower in American foreign relations," according to the former director of public affairs. [21] The term "public affairs" replaced "public information" to emphasize that the opinion-policy relationship was a two-way street. The bipartisan consensus on collective security that Hull had so delicately assembled was not to be sacrificed by provoking congressional resentment of "government propaganda."

If Congress could be relied upon to approve the broad lines of Stettinius's reforms the same could not be said for his choice of nominees, especially in the highly charged public information field. Archibald MacLeish, the Librarian of Congress and former director of the Office of Facts and Figures, did not construe his proposed assignment as one limited to "public relations." On the contrary, he made it very clear to Stettinius that his acceptance of the nomination for assistant secretary was premised on the assumption of a real role in the policy-making process. When word of his impending nomination leaked out the press speculated, to MacLeish's intense annoyance, that he had been chosen as a kind of "public relations expert" who was supposed to come in "after the policies are made to sell them to the country—or anyway to try to sell them to the liberals." [22] This was not at all what he had in mind: "One of the most difficult things I will have to do will be to make it clear to my colleagues in the department that the Assistant Secretary in charge of public and cultural relations is a policy making official of the department in the same sense and to the same degree as the other Assistant Secretaries." MacLeish told the secretary, "You and I understand each other on this point perfectly." [23]

MacLeish's conception of the public information function as an integral part of the policy process did seem to accord with Stettinius's outlook. The secretary had spoken to MacLeish, in a characteristic corporate metaphor, of *all* the assistant secretaries as board members with one vote each. He reassured MacLeish that his colleagues in the department and elsewhere in government would "know soon enough that your role is not merely 'Public Relations Counsellor.'"[24]

MacLeish was a controversial nominee and Stettinius, almost simultaneously, was assuring other intimates of his determination to keep the poet out of policy. Responding to Mrs. Hull's doubts he told her: "If we can control MacLeish and keep him out of policy, I think it will be all right."[25] This was probably no more than a mark of deference to her husband who had not always enjoyed the best relations with MacLeish. Joseph Davies warned that MacLeish might try to make use of his personal White House connections and advised the secretary that all clearance should be through him.

The press and members of the Senate took up these and other criticism. The *Chicago Tribune*, scarcely a friend of the administration, had this to say:

> The new organization, it is reported, will be "brainstrusted" by Archibald MacLeish, poet and Librarian of Congress. MacLeish's

name is before the Senate for confirmation as an assistant secretary of state. He is said to have been chosen to preside over a great propaganda machine to influence public opinion at home and abroad in favor of various global plans by which the President and Harry Hopkins hope to extend the New Deal thruout the world.[26]

As Inis Claude demonstrates, one need not be an isolationist to perceive the United Nations as the "classical expression" of the kind of liberalism that gave rise to the New Deal.[27] The plausibility of the analogy, and so the hostility of the "irreconcilables" in the Senate, was increased by the bureaucratic history of opinion-influencing agencies and the personal history of MacLeish. Many of OWI's predecessors, such as the USIS, had begun as disseminators of information about the National Recovery Program and other aspects of the New Deal.

On December 4, Stettinius visited Senator Tom Connally, chairman of the Senate Foreign Relations Committee, to allay such fears about MacLeish and his fellow nominees.[28] In Connally's office Stettinius met Senators Wallace H. White and Arthur Vandenberg. Vandenberg told him he thought MacLeish was terrible and that ten senators already had spoken to him about it.[29] Somewhat chastened, the secretary resolved to tell MacLeish about these objections to him and, perhaps, not to play up his role in policy.

The next day Senators White, Vandenberg, and Clark did vote against MacLeish's nomination in the Foreign Relations Committee, but their opposition was insufficient to prevent Connally from reporting out the whole slate of nominations to the Senate. Very dissatisfied, Senator Clark, then lame-duck senator from Missouri, decided to fight and demanded open hearings on MacLeish, whom he regarded with deep suspicion.[30] A majority of the Senate went even further and refused to confirm *any* of the nominees without open committee hearings.

Arthur Krock explained the Senate's unprecedented action in overruling the favorable report in terms of the desire of certain groups within the Senate to reassert legislative prerogatives in foreign affairs. Conservative and New Deal Democrats alike saw the hand of Harry Hopkins behind the nominations. According to Krock, they wished to signal their displeasure to the president at the formulation of foreign policy by White House cabal.[31]

With the nominations back in committee, the secretary loyally defended his proposed colleagues despite sustained innuendo. He took up the theme of the interdependence between an informed public and a workable postwar settlement in justifying MacLeish's appointment: "I believe that the new problems involved in making a secure peace require that much fuller information about United States foreign policy should be made available through the established press, radio and other media both to the people of this country and the people of other countries."[32] MacLeish's experience as a soldier, lawyer, editor, writer and Librarian of Congress "ideally qualif[ied]" him for the job of seeing that this was done.

Predictably, Senator Clark did not agree. He took MacLeish back over his service as director of OFF and as Librarian of Congress: "Did you consider it was part of your duties," he asked, ". . . to be an active propagandist in the United States with respect to matters of public policy and to criticize the policy of Congress and, to some extent, the policy of the State Department?"[33] MacLeish assured him that he did not and that, in any event, his new duties were entirely different. The *New York Times* backed him up on this not by arguing that he lacked the deficiencies to which the senator referred but by suggesting that in his new position they might prove to be virtues: At OFF "the criticism was that instead of merely supplying the American people with facts and figures, he conducted democratic psychological warfare with his data and looked at it primarily from the angle of his preconceived opinions how the public ought to react. But this attitude, assuming he still has it, will be less objectionable if his job is to tell the administration story of foreign policy as the frank propagandist such functionaries are expected to be."[34]

Senator Clark's initial questions followed the general pattern that had been evident in the OWI hearings of the previous summer: an attempt to substantiate the fear that direct links between presidential agents and the people inherently undermined the representative authority of the legislature in foreign affairs. But the next day he launched into an altogether more vituperative attack on MacLeish's work and, more insidiously, on his political sympathies. In a style of interrogation that foreshadowed the McCarthy hearings, attempts were made to link MacLeish with various communist and fellow-traveling organizations of the 1930s and to cast aspersion on his support for the Loyalists in Spain. Most of the attacks, rather transparently, depended on quotations out of context and on unsubstantiated reports.[35]

Perhaps the purpose was no more than to elicit professions of loyalty to the American republic and its political and economic institutions. If so, the interrogations were successful. Senator Albert B. Chandler valiantly extracted from the nominee the confession that he had not only written poetry but had also played football at Yale and that he had fought in World War I at the Battle of the Marne. Finally, at midnight on December 13, after several tied votes, the committee confirmed MacLeish.

BANISHING SPECTERS OF THE PAST

Why did public opinion figure so prominently in the State Depatment's formulation of collective security policy? It did so, this study suggests, because of a common assumption that past failures of collective security could be attributed to the inadequate preparation of public opinion. Modern scholars, soured by the application of the appeasement analogy to communism in Southeast Asia, are apt to turn Santayana on his head: "Too often," they write, "it is those who *can* remember the past who are condemned to repeat it." [36] But there is no evidence that any of the planners who conferred about postwar policy in 1944 doubted the wisdom of the original aphorism.

First, there was the desire to avoid at all costs a repeat of the 1919 fiasco, which many attributed to Wilson's insensitivity to the nuances of public and congressional opinion. This view was expressed in a secret memorandum, which passed between the president and the secretary of state in May 1944. In the last war, it recalled, "there was very little public discussion before the armistice on that policies and what machinery should be adopted to win the peace. The absence of an informed public opinion on this subject was probably not without its effects in the failure to get adequate Congressional and public support for the League." [37] This "lesson of the past" permeated the entire policy-making apparatus. Dickey told the present author that the men who worked on the drafting and public presentation of the Dumbarton Oaks proposals were all determined "not to pull another Woodrow Wilson." [38] To them this meant not to pursue collective security without allowing time for a supporting public consensus to develop. Cast in positive terms the 1919 analogy contained the imperative to seek actively such a consensus using the new machinery that Stettinius had created at State. MacLeish told a radio audience of more than ten million that the most satisfying aspect of the Yalta conference was that it drew lessons from the past: "This time we're not waiting for a peace conference to set up [a permanent international organization]. We made that mistake last time. We tried to run the war and the peace last time in two sections, and it didn't work."[39] His words illustrate the policy maker's concern to profit from the past and his determination to use the air waves to make sure that the public did so too.

Of course it was not the public en masse but the Senate that proved to be Wilson's stumbling block. Here was the major lesson the White House culled from the League of Nations fiasco in 1919:

> As Roosevelt and others saw it, Wilson had made three mistakes. He had failed to involve the Senate in drafting the Covenant. He had antagonized the Republicans and made the League a party issue. And he had banked on post-war continuation of wartime idealism. In all three respects Roosevelt sought to do exactly the opposite.[40]

He did so by striking while the iron was hot, without waiting for the peace to cool legislative enthusiasm. House and Senate leaders were brought into the drafting and negotiating process whenever possible. The nervousness of some members of the State Foreign Relations Committee pointed to the need for close liaison. This reached its culmination in Vandenberg's vocal presence on the American delegation to the San Francisco conference. In the House, the passage by a large bipartisan majority of 360 to 29 of William Fulbright's resolution reduced the risk of a repetition of Wilson's second mistake. The resolution declared:

> That the Congress hereby expersses itself as favoring the creation of appropriate international machinery adequate to establish and maintain a just and lasting peace among the nations of the world, and as favoring participation by the United States therein.

In the Senate, the internationalist ginger group around Ball, Burton, Hatch, and Hill was, if anything, more advanced in its view than the administration. "By co-opting Senators and Republican leaders," as May puts it, "Roosevelt might get American membership in a world organization."[41] A Gallup survey in July 1943 showed that the American people approved the Fulbright formula by a margin of 78 percent to 9 percent, with 13 percent expressing no opinion.[42]

With favorable pluralities of this order in Congress and among the public wherein lay the need for a massive campaign to educate the public? There are two answers to this question. The first lies in another historical analogy, which seemed even more compelling than the 1919 case: the failure of appeasement and collective security in the 1930s. Chapter 2 showed that the State Department blamed the isolationist stance of the American public for the weakness of America's earlier stand against the Axis.[43] The second answer lies in the nature of the proposed security organization: it was one thing for the public to support the general principle and another for it to come to a realistic and informed understanding of what collective security meant. We shall consider each in turn.

Just as generals plan to fight the last war, the proponents of collective security planned to prevent it. In March 1945, Under Secretary of State Grew told a radio audience: "There is no doubt in my mind that the Security Council would act if we were faced again by the kind of situations which arose in Germany and in Italy under Hitler and Mussolini before the war. And this time we would take action before a war started."[44] The very concept of "collective security" was redolent of the 1930s and the failure of the League.[45] Since that failure was generally assumed to have been, in part, the result of the isolationism of the American public, it became imperative to guard against a resurgence of isolationism. A compelling part of the lesson drawn from the vacillations of the age of appeasement was the critical importance of disabusing the public of its isolationist illusions by means of a bold public-information strategy.

Early wartime surveys suggested that the internationalist drift in popular opinion might have been a wartime aberration, springing more from emotion than from conviction or understanding. As such, its intensity and durability could not be taken for granted. Most congressional bastions of isolationism survived the 1944 elections, strengthening the government's need to bolster the emerging bipartisan consensus. As early as January 1943, the Political Subcommittee, a postwar policy group usually chaired by Hull, Welles, or Berle, identified retreat into isolationism as a *potential* tendency that the government had to combat. Otherwise there was a risk that the committee's imaginative and, at the time, seemingly visionary plans might be too far in advance of public opinion. "Concerning the growing interest on the part of the American public in post-war problems in general," the minutes of January 30 record,

> it was suggested that the strength of isolationist opinion would be an important factor to take into account in the near future. It was hoped that while the subcommittee was working out a constructive program for the post-war world, it would not find itself in the position of not being supported by public opinion. [46]

One way to reduce the risk of this was to concentrate on the "realistic" interests served by collective security rather than the apparently altruistic U.N. ideal. The decision to turn away from world government in favor of a more limited peace-keeping organization not only accorded with Roosevelt's predisposition but also reflected the fear of resurgent isolationism. This is an example of the impact of public opinion in determining the feasibility of a foreign-policy option. [47] This influence assumed a more tangible form in contributing to the American position on the voting formula at Dumbarton Oaks and Yalta.

But during the spring of 1943 it meant no more than a presentation of collective security to the public as a means of securing vital national interests. This, it was hoped, would be the antidote to isolationist and anti-New Deal disparagement of political "altruism." Plans had not yet crystallized into the United Nations; policy discussions were cast in terms of greater American participation in the League of Nations. [48]

Two strategies were proposed, one for dealing with America's allies and one for informing the American public. The first would emphasize the unconditional fact of America's emergence on the world scene: "The problem is not whether the United States will be willing to assume responsibility for post-war arrangements, but whether it will be allowed to do so in areas where it has vital interests." The second, addressed to the American public, would take up the same theme, pointing out that if the United States did not assert its interests in the settlement, it might become "beleaguered on all sides and placed in a dangerously weak position." [49] This could be avoided if the country followed the principles of security, welfare, and justice. An international organization based on these principles would require "no surrender of American traditions." While it asserted its interests America would limit its responsibilities and so alleviate fears that its allies were taking advantage of American generosity.

Some revisionist historians argue that America's approach to the postwar settlement was predicated upon the need to avoid an economic recession, with its turbulent political consequences in Europe and the United States.[50] Although these meetings of the Political Subcommittee in the spring of 1943 have not been cited in support of this view they might very easily serve the purpose, especially if quoted in brief. For example, in April Sumner Welles told the group that

> some Americans were said to fear that the United States will be expected to do "all the co-operating" and to feed, clothe, reconstruct, and police the world. It will be necessary to convince the public that the government's program is not altruistic but that it has two very practical objectives: to safeguard American security by providing free access to raw materials and fostering international commerce.[51]

Here, apparently unadorned, is William A. Williams's "open door policy" appearing as a rationale for collective security.[52] But in fact, the stress on equal access to raw materials and free trade did not emerge from cabals of the power elite but rather from efforts to appease the economic nationalism of the American people. The administration's postwar policy was formulated and adapted in accordance with the perceived requirements of public consent.

Nor were policy makers without evidence from the polls. A month after the plans for a United Nations were laid in Moscow, Hadley Cantril reported to the White House disturbing evidence of the public's parochialism. He sent an index comparing public interest in domestic and international affairs to Judge Samuel Rosenman who probably passed it on to Stettinius.[53] Cantril summarized this index by saying, "People are almost twice as much interested in domestic affairs." Other questions— and it must be said they were rather leading questions—elicited the public's view on postwar aid programs: 45 percent believed that if the United States were to furnish "all necessary aid to friendly countries after the war" the standard of living in America would be lowered; 31 percent thought it would remain the same while 10 percent, perhaps anticipating the practice of tied aid, thought American living standards would be raised; 10 percent had no opinion.[54]

For policy makers anxious about a resurgence of isolationism, these findings contained a clear message, which Cantril spelled out under the heading, "Suggested Procedure to Make Administration's Post-War Policy Acceptable to American Public":

> Solely as a method for obtaining support for its international plans, the administration should carefully avoid giving the impression to the nation that foreign affairs will be carried on at the expense of domestic progress.
>
> Wherever possible, in all public statements, the administration should tie all references to international cooperation clearly and closely to the public's own self-interest here at home.
>
> It should be pointed out that the people's ultimate welfare will be further advanced by international cooperation than by inaction on our part. [55]

So the basic decision was taken, during 1943, that postwar policy, and especially the United Nations, was to be presented not primarily in idealistic terms but in terms capable of convincing even a hardened America Firster. A meeting of the State Department's Political Subcommittee concluded that "attention should be concentrated on two main objectives: the need to prevent wars and to provide access to raw materials. The people should be shown that they have important benefits to receive from an international organization; and they should be convinced, while the lessons of war are still before them, that they have global interests and responsibilities."[56]

These plans, with their unmistakable stamp of Hull's views on foreign economic policy, were not without ambiguities. The people were to be educated to their world responsibilities but reassured about the limits of those responsibilities. They were to be wooed in the language of internationalism but reminded that behind every ideal stood an interest. A major challenge to the public-opinion specialist was to overcome the prejudices of the past and the very natural desire to return to local and domestic pursuits, without overstepping the bounds of realism.

The inculcation of a realistic and informed understanding of the meaning of collective security was the second problem facing public affairs specialists. By August 1944 when the Dumbarton Oaks conference met, the "triumph of internationalism,"[57] was by no means assured. Neither the general public, the press, the Congress, nor promotional groups had any doubt about the *principle* of collective security; disagreement and uncertainty focused on its structure and powers. The level of general approval of American participation in an international security organization, and its rate of growth is suggested by table 13, which the State Department prepared for the delegates attending the San Francisco conference. [58] But once the issue became more complex than the general principle of international organization, confusion and uncertainty became evident among the public and, indeed, in Congress and the administration. The principle of an international police force won wide approval but "most Americans [had] no very clear idea of how an international police force works. [59] People were unsure of the relationship between such a force and national military organizations. Large majorities favored compulsory military service in the postwar period but could not decide whether the resultant military establishments should be stronger, weaker, or equivalent to forces at the disposal of the United Nations (see table 14).

Despite these uncertainties, it did not seem in 1944 that the majority of the public would approve of Hull's plan to have the United Nations keep the peace "by force if necessary," even while they clung to a strong American military establishment. This was also the position of most organized promotional groups. [60] The police force question was critical during the policy formulation stage; it was a simple metaphor which Roosevelt liked to use in his speeches. But in practice the question was moot since the U.N.'s military staff committee never became operational.

Polls indicated that the public was prepared to assign a number of other powers to the world organization, including the right to assess

TABLE 13
Would You Like to See the United States Join a League of Nations?

		Yes	*No*	*No Opinion*
October	1937	26%	52%	22%
May	1941	37	39	24
November	1942	55	20	25
October	1943	62	17	21
April	1944	70	14	16
June	1944	72	13	15

Source: AIPO Polls, 1937, 1941, 1942, 1944 (June), OPOR Polls, 1943, 1944 (April).

TABLE 14

However Large the U.S. Army Will Be After the War, Do You Think the International Police Force Should be Larger, Smaller, or about the Same Size?

Larger	32%
Smaller	25
Same	20
No opinion	23

Source: AIPO Poll, September 1943.

members' contributions, to stipulate permissible levels of military preparations by members, to formulate international law, and, in general, to prevent the outbreak of war. These findings indicated an astonishingly permissive attitude on the part of the public. State Department planners grew more and more convinced that they needed to inject a powerful dose of realism into the public debate. Otherwise, it was feared, disenchantment would rapidly lead to a reversion to isolationism.

The Dumbarton Oaks conference provided the first major opportunity for the reorganized State Department to make a substantial contribution to public understanding of the emerging pattern of the postwar world. Despite his previous public-relations experience the conference bred in Stettinius "great personal frustration" in contending with "the public demand for information."[61] Here "the public" really meant the press, for whom the American delegation had made almost no provisions at Dumbarton Oaks. The conference was held in an aura of great secrecy; the under secretary was bound by a decision of all the conferees that no separate press statements would be made. But the American delegation had not even considered public information strategy at all; it included no representative of the new Office of Public Information. Instead Michael McDermott served as the delegation's tight-lipped press officer.

Stettinius's deference to the agreed principle of secrecy was not shared by all the delegations, and on August 23 James Reston was able to publish a detailed account of the proceedings gleaned from Chinese sources. Similar embarrassments occurred the following year at the San Francisco conference where American reporters were forced to sniff around other delegations for details of the American position.

Archibald MacKenzie, press officer of the British delegation, told correspondents that he regretted their rather offhand treatment and that he hoped a more liberal press policy could be worked out. The following day, August 24, in what the *New York Times* called a "combined démarche," representatives of the press corps were received by the three delegations. This was the product of the embarrassment caused by Reston's scoop. The press continued to grumble about secrecy after their reception, and the barriers surrounding the Georgetown mansion were compared with those around a concentration camp.[62] Finally, six days after the Reston story, Stettinius issued a tactful but firm statement pointing out that an atmosphere of confidentiality was essential if the Allies were to make substantial progress toward agreement.[63]

TAKING OUT THE WORD

After this the immediate secrecy issue died down, although it had further ramifications. If the press could not be kept up to date with the government's position, how could the kind of informed public opinion deemed indispensable by Hull emerge? Dickey recalls that after Dumbarton Oaks a meeting was called between Stettinius, Pasvolsky, Alger Hiss, and Edwin Wilson (director of the Office of Special Political Affairs; Hiss was his assistant). An "atmosphere of crisis" prevailed at the meeting whose purpose was to devise a better approach to public liaison.

A plan was devised to "take out the word" of the Dumbarton Oaks agreements to the mass public and to organized groups, including those whose purpose was basically apolitical. For one of the consequences of "secrecy" was plain public ignorance about the content and the very existence of the agreements. A study conducted by the Office of Public Affairs on the basis of data supplied by Cantril found that in December 1944 only 43 percent of respondents had "heard or read of the Dumbarton Oaks Proposals" while 57 percent could not identify them at all.[64] Another purpose of a new public-information effort was to restore the department's luster, which the secrecy affair had tarnished.

Preservation of the bipartisan nature of the internationalist movement provided an additional impetus to the State Department group's determination to "take out the word." Governor Thomas Dewey of New York had pledged his support to the administration's foreign policy, and, for the most part, postwar issues were kept out of the presidential election campaign.[65] (Despite this moratorium Roosevelt did manage to link the Republicans with isolationism in the last weeks of the campaign.)[66] During the Dumbarton Oaks conversations Dewey's foreign policy adviser, John Foster Dulles, said that he favored fuller information being made available to the public.[67] Other Republican leaders whom Hull had recruited were, in Dickey's words, "scared and wanted to make sure of public support."[68] It was almost a quid pro quo for Republican support that the administration undertook to mobilize public consent and to keep collective security out of politics. Only then could skeptical opposition leaders have confidence that there would be no electoral backlash against their accommodations with Roosevelt and Hull.

On November 20, Stettinius distributed a publicity package to newsmen to aid in public understanding. It consisted of an organizational chart, a popular device in the department, and a series of questions and answers. The under secretary said that the package was part of the public education program then being conducted through meetings in Washington with representative groups and in talks by department officers throughout the country. "The aim," he said, "was to inform the public on the plan before the full United Nations Conference meets to vote the Charter in its final form."[69] In contrast to the 1919 situation, this period of public discussion would, he hoped, allow time for the feeling to grow that the organization was a collective endeavor in which all had a stake. By stressing the tentative nature of the proposals he tried to give the public a sense of their own capacity to influence the final outcome.

An example of this consultative-educative process can be seen in the meeting held at the Department of State on October 16 between officials and representatives of Americans United for World Organization and the Commission to Study the Organization for Peace. Representatives of more than ninety groups, by no means restricted to "internationalists," assembled to take part in off-the-record briefings and to listen to an address by Stettinius in which he declared his willingness to invite "critical and candid" scrutiny of the proposals. He repeated the department's conventional wisdom on the democratic formulation of foreign policy, which, by then, had become almost an incantation:

> Only as there develops in this country a substantial and informed body of public opinion can the government go forward successfully in the task of participation in the further steps needed for the es-

tablishment of an international organization. Only against the background of such a body of public opinion can the organization itself once established function effectively; for no institution, however perfect, can live and fulfill its purpose unless it is continuously animated and supported by strong public will and determination. [70]

This theme was hammered home time and again during the fall and early winter of 1944. Its prominence not only in public pronouncements but also in secluded strategy sessions rules out the argument that it was no more than rhetorical cant.

Roosevelt's victory in the 1944 election by no means disposed of the fear that a version to isolationism might set in among the public and in Congress. It was still true

> that Hiram Johnson, one of the "Irreconcilables" of 1919, remained a senior member of the Senate Foreign Relations Committee; that the sponsor of the Neutrality laws, Senator Gerald Nye, was still around; that Robert A. Taft of Ohio, last ditch opponent of Lend-Lease, had been runner-up for the 1944 Republican Presidential nomination; and that newspapers in the Hearst and Gannett chains, Mrs. Patterson's *Washington Times Herald* and *New York Daily News* and Colonel McCormick's *Chicago Tribune* expressed views similar to those of Johnson, Nye and Taft and reached tens of millions of readers. [71]

This did not look like an opposition that could be readily discounted.

Public-opinion polls analyzed by the Office of Public Affairs showed that by December 57 percent of Cantril's respondents still had not heard or read of the Dumbarton Oaks proposals. [72] This was alarming in light of the department's exertions throughout the fall and seemed to call for more concerted action. There was some comfort in the continued general approval of American participation in an international organization of some kind. By April 1945 "8 out of 10 Americans favor[ed] joining an international organization to maintain peace by the use of force if necessary." [73]

The elevation of public affairs and the advent of MacLeish were designed, in part, to deepen this surface support. Strategy sessions in the secretary's staff committee, an innovation of the December shake-up, revealed a kind of intuitive grasp of what Katz and Lazarsfeld were to describe as "the two-step flow of communication," [74] the hypothesis that "ideas often flow *from* radio and print *to* the opinion leaders, and from them to the less active sections of the population." If this were the case economy demanded a concentration of educational effort on the opinion leaders—the strategy implicitly followed during the fall. But such was the intensity of belief in the need to mobilize not only the elite but also the mass public that a two-pronged information strategy, targeted at both strata, was adopted. This resulted in what even some practitioners of the policy have conceded was oversell or overkill. [75]

But this was not apparent until much later and remains the subject of a certain amount of controversy. [76] At the time it was not oversell but isolationism that rose as a specter before opinion analysts. By February Cantril reported that a dent had been made in the percentage unaware of the proposals: it fell from 57 percent in December 1944 to 48 percent in February, and was to fall to 40 percent in March. [77] But of the 60 percent who were aware of the proposals in March only 28 percent thought that they "provided a real and practical basis for setting up an international organization to maintain world peace." [78] Nine percent of this informed group thought that the proposals did not provide such a basis, while 23 percent had no opinion.

The need to deepen popular understanding and support coexisted with the need to eradicate simplistic beliefs. How to stimulate enthusiasm while tempering optimism with the increasingly gloomy realities of international politics? Conflicts between the great powers were to be avoided but official publicity must not pretend that a collective security organization could itself prevent war in the event of such a conflict. The absence of conflict between the members of the Grand Alliance could be only an illusion in the months following Yalta. So even a balanced public-information program was encouraging the public to stake its hopes on a situation of amity which had ceased to exist. [79]

These cross-pressures were evident in the formulation of the crucial information campaign, which culminated in the San Francisco conference. MacLeish summarized the principles of the campaign as follows:

1. That one thing we do believe in is that an international organization offers the only practical means of preventing war.
2. That the Dumbarton Oaks proposals are a means to that end.

3. That the department welcomes criticism of the proposals but that in view of the way in which they were worked out, the burden of proof is on the critics.
4. That the department must be candid in telling the people of the limitations of the proposals as well as their possibilities. [80]

MacLeish's third point can be understood in terms of the multistage decision process outlined in chapter 1. The agitation of internationalist groups had contributed to the first stage: identification of the issue. The impact of the general public had been felt at the second and third stages: specification of policy options and selection of desired policy. It had fed into the decision through the canvassing of mass opinion. Now at the fourth stage, implementation, it was up to the government to take the initiative in mobilizing support. The burden of proof was on the critics; opinion had already been transmitted to policy makers and incorporated in their decision at an earlier and less visible stage in the policy process.

The fourth point in the public information program contained the heart of the matter. Leo Pasvolsky felt very strongly that the public ought not to be presented with a masquerade concerning the realities of great power conflict. He repeatedly argued that everyone should be made to understand that if a great power wanted to start a war no machinery could stop it. This point crystallized in the debate over voting procedure at Yalta and San Francisco. At the urging of Pasvolsky MacLeish undertook to add the following to the fourth guiding principle in the government's public information program:

The Department feels that the American people should understand that the proposed organization *would* not in itself and of itself stop all wars. Specifically, it *would* not stop a war initiated by, or favored by one of the Great Powers. [81]

Nelson Rockefeller was "startled by the frankness of this statement" [82] and thought that it contradicted point 1. Stettinius temporized by proposing that the "would" be replaced by "might."

Dean Acheson, then the senior assistant secretary of state, thought that a candid account of the limitations of the new organization was difficult since "we start with a generalization which is not true and then feel that we must say something to offset this. We make the illogical state-

ment that we must go to war to prevent war." His resolution of the
dilemma amounted to little more than a characteristic display of verbal
gymnastics: "If we say that the new organization is the embryo of order
in the world we can avoid this difficulty."[83]

On February 10, 1945, MacLeish presented a revised statement of information policy which conceded that the people should be informed
that disputes between great powers and disputes between small powers
might have a different status as far as the prevention of war was concerned. The department should publicize this point "on its own motion
and not by way of explanation or defense." It should also be conceded
that the maintenance of good relations between the great powers was a
necessary condition for the success of the proposals.[84]

A PUBLIC-RELATIONS BLITZKRIEG

How far did these meticulous discussions of public-information policy
correspond with the picture of the world body that actually reached the
public? We shall try to answer this question by examining the content of
samples of the information transmitted to the public between the time of
MacLeish's appointment and the San Francisco conference, which convened on April 25, 1945. During this period the Department of State
employed a varied battery of information instruments. Its media of
communications with the public included:[85]

1. Film.   — A film of the Dumbarton Oaks proposals featuring
                the Secretary of State, made under the auspices of
                the War Activities Committee of the Motion Picture
                Industry.
2. Radio.   — Overall coordination by OWI's radio bureau.
             — A "fact sheet" for the guidance of broadcasters.
             — A pamphlet for mass distribution to aid in answering
                listeners' questions.
             — A State Department radio series, featuring leading
                officers, beginning on February 24, and continuing
                until the eve of the San Francisco conference.
3. Public speaking.
             — Nationwide tours by Department and Foreign
                Service Officers.

4. Magazine advertising.
5. Publications.

"Generally speaking," the planning document sums up, "steps have been taken to mobilize the principal media of communication in the United States for the prupose of bringing to the people of the country in the next eight to ten weeks the information they require with respect to various proposals for the peace."

No doubt all this did amount to a "public-relations blitzkrieg."[86] Stettinius himself referred to the program as "an aggressive policy for public relations."[87] But throughout the blitzkrieg equally strenuous steps were taken to acquaint the department with public reactions, doubts, and uncertainties. Late in 1944, Dickey's office had begun preparing a fortnightly survey of opinion, analyzing editorial and public sentiment. Throughout the "campaign" it was MacLeish's custom to read the latest trends to the secretary's staff committee. Minutes of its meetings indicate that discussion was often keyed to the revealed fluctuations in public response. Stettinius would forward poll data to the president when it seemed to be of pressing concern.[88] The flow of data to the White House along Cantril's informal channel also continued.

The two-way flow of opinion is illustrated by the president's preoccupation with the subject as he departed for Yalta. "The President's advisers had public opinion much on their minds as they prepared for Yalta," Gaddis writes. "A summary of opinion polls sent to Roosevelt early in January concluded that recent events 'have increased public skepticism concerning the ability of the major powers to live up to the ideals of the Atlantic Charter and the United Nations.'"[89] Gaddis argues that even the selection of advisers to accompany the president was influenced by the configuration of public opinion. James Byrnes was chosen as a man sufficiently independent of the president (a southern democrat whom Roosevelt had not put on the 1944 ticket, despite his standing with the party) for his word to carry weight with the Congress.

FILM

On December 8, 1944, Francis Harmon, chairman of the War Activities Committee of the Motion Picture Industry, approached Stettinius about making a film on postwar American foreign policy.[90] The secretary responded positively finding that Elmer Davis—still at OWI—was in favor of the project.[91]

Plans went ahead rapidly under the guidance of Francis Harmon. The public affairs people contacted Alfred Hitchcock, who agreed to direct the film, and Ben Hecht, the playwright, then under contract to Twentieth Century Fox, who undertook to write the script. Hitchcock and Hecht arrived in Washington on December 26 and sat up most of the night roughing out a script. The next day Hecht read the script to an august meeting in the Department of State, including the secretary. "Everybody thought [the script] was an excellent job," Stettinius noted. [92] It "dealt with the proposed international organization in dramatic form by projecting into the future and telling the story of its operation in stopping an unnamed potential aggressor about the year 1960." [93]

Alfred Hitchcock suggested, no doubt with great tact, that the dramatic effect might be diminished if the secretary insisted on a planned six- or seven-minute speech on the screen. This was a technique that had been popular in wartime; it had been used, for example, in Joseph Davies's film glorifying the Soviet Union, *Mission to Moscow*. The impact would be far greater, Hitchcock thought, if the secretary narrated the entire film, making only a *brief* appearance.

The film, "Watchtower over Tomorrow," did not go into production immediately for there were policy objections within the department. The question of voting procedure in the Security Council had not yet been settled with the Soviet Union. Pasvolsky thought that realism demanded that the film should make clear that the "unnamed aggressor" was not one of the great powers. While such problems were debated in the department, production was delayed. MacLeish cabled Harmon to release Hitchcock and Hecht from work on the film while the policy makers made up their minds. [94]

Pasvolsky's criticism was dispatched to Hecht in Hollywood, who did his best to incorporate it into the script, which would specify that the "unnamed aggressor" was not a permanent member of the Security Council. Meanwhile the secretary of state visited the Twentieth Century Fox studios in New York City on January 12 to make his debut. "They took all day just to do these three minutes," Wilder Foote records. "Mr. Stettinius did no acting. He sat at his desk, walked to the fireplace and walked towards the camera while he was speaking." [95]

Hitchcock made the rest of the film in Hollywood. Francis Russell, who succeeded Dickey as director of the Office of Public Affairs in 1945, was sent from the department to supervise the shooting. Foote noted, "I fear there is too much chance of the film's going wrong on important policy points, especially with the combined imaginations of Messrs. Hecht and Hitchcock at work." [96] After various editing sessions the film was ready for distribution in April, on the eve of the San Francisco conference.

The majority of press opinion was favorable, although an editorial in the *New York Daily News* said that the film was "laying the propaganda on too thick." [97] A none-too-scientific report from OWI forwarded some observations of audience reaction. Although one Washington patron complained that he had already seen the film three times, slipped in before various features, other patrons rejoined that they had not seen the film before and that the subject matter was intensely interesting. [98] In a pretelevision prelude to Lazy Shave politics, Drew Pearson commented on the shiftiness of the secretary's eyes. But Stettinius's loyal subordinate, Wilder Foote, reassured him: "I do not think the shifting of your eyes in your appearance in the film was noticeable or disturbing except at one point. In a medium close-up you rolled your eyes upward, evidently to catch the script. However, immediately afterwards in the final close-up, you looked straight at the audience and did a beautiful job with your last few lines." [99]

Looking back over this chapter one of the protagonists says of "Watchtower over Tomorrow" that "as the apogee of the Department's effort to take this foreign policy to the 'people,' it is an historical exhibit meriting study more than emulation." [100]

RADIO

On December 27, 1944, Sterling Fisher of NBC proposed to Secretary Stettinius a series of radio programs on international peace and security. [101] Fischer made his suggestion the same day that Stettinius met with Hecht, Hitchcock, and the others on the film project. The new secretary was fired with the potential of the mass media and very soon elicited an affirmative recommendation from MacLeish and Dickey. A series of seven broadcasts was scheduled on Saturday evenings between February 24 and April 7. As in the previous year's broadcasts, "The State Department Speaks," "Our Foreign Policy" served a dual purpose: it presented the security issues involved at Dumbarton Oaks, Yalta, and San Francisco to the public in as colloquial and comprehensible way as MacLeish and his colleagues could manage; and also, in the wake of Stettinius's administrative reforms, it continued the drive to restore the

State Department to hegemony in the foreign-policy bureaucracy by presenting the department's revitalized, new image. This dual purpose can be gauged from the titles of some of the programs: "America's Foreign Policy," "Main Street and Dumbarton Oaks," and "It's Your State Depatment." [102]

Archibald MacLeish was the moderator of all the broadcasts. He told his audience, which ranged from ten million to fifteen million, that he would act as a public interrogator, channeling questions sent in by listeners to high State Department personnel. [103] In this way the diffusion of information would be linked to the transmission of the public's doubts and uncertainties. MacLeish's questions did indeed provide this linkage, although with rather less ingenuousness than his folksy presentation suggested. The questions were, of course, designed to permit the victims of his probing to answer along the lines of the main informational themes, which had been agreed on in the planning sessions at the beginning of February. These specific themes about the United Nations were interlaced with efforts to dispel popular prejudices about the department and with invocations of domestic opinion as the cornerstone of a democratic foreign policy.

The programs were broadcast during the "false dawn" of postwar cooperation, which followed the Yalta conference. At times they reflect a painful strain for consistency between Soviet-American friendship and the increasingly harsh realities of politics in Eastern Europe. It had become an explicit assumption of MacLeish's information strategy that such friendship was a necessary condition for the success of the United Nations.

In addition to mail from the public, the program was keyed to public reaction to the Yalta decisions as gauged by the Division of Public Liaison in Dickey's office. Initially, the Yalta declaration met with an enthusiastic response from the press and the public. Disquiet centered on Poland's political and territorial future. [104] Doubts on this score were, to some extent, counterbalanced by the visible evidence of Allied cooperation in the agreement of Britain, the U.S.S.R., and the United States to attend the San Francisco conference and to invite delegates from all the United Nations. New doubts about Soviet-American cooperation were raised by the piecemeal release of certain agreements not included in the original declaration: the requirement for great power unanimity in the Security Council, announced on March 5, and the agreement to separate seats in the General Assembly for the Ukraine and White Russia, announced on March 29.[105]

McDermott, the State Department's press officer, attacked each of these problems as they arose with off-the-record briefings and a press conference by the secretary. On the broadcast "It's Your State Department," he explained the difficulty these developments posed for information officers. The "extra seats" issue was, to some extent, defused by the announcement that Stettinius had negotiated similar rights for the United States but that the president, magnanimously, had chosen not to exercise the right. As for unanimity, or "the veto," McDermott pointed out that it was required for enforcement and even peaceful action to settle a dispute but not, as many feared, for the discussion of a dispute.[106]

Dean Acheson seized his opportunity to address some of these issues on the first program of the series. The two most significant accomplishments of the Yalta conference, he said, were the completion of the Dumbarton Oaks proposals and agreement on the treatment of Germany. MacLeish thought that the single most significant achievement at Yalta was progress toward a permanent security organization.[107] This achievement was notable not only from an international perspective—the preservation of Allied unity and the willingness to compromise—but also from the perspective of domestic opinion:

> Acheson: The great majority of Americans want to join as soon as possible a world organization to preserve the peace.
>
> MacLeish: I'd say that that objective was reflected in the decisions of the Crimea Conference wouldn't you?
>
> Acheson: Yes, the results of that conference were in complete harmony with American opinion. That explains why the Conference was so widely acclaimed.[108]

In a disquisition on the public's impact on foreign policy Acheson conveyed the impression that American diplomats and statesmen generally did little more than to carry the popular will beyond the water's edge. "How much difference is there between foreign policy and domestic policy from the point of view of public opinion?" MacLeish asked him. "Do you think that foreign policy lags behind public opinion more than domestic policy?" "I think there is no difference," Acheson replied.

"Foreign policy in a democracy is merely the expression of the people's purpose with reference to matters outside the nation, whereas domestic policy is concerned with matters inside the nation."[109] This version of the opinion-policy relationship, so similar to the official interpretation of the impact of public opinion during the 1930s, was tendentious, to say the least, in the context of the Yalta accords. Public-opinion reports indicated that vocal minorities were extremely distressed at the proposed territorial settlement of the Polish question and at the vagueness of Stalin's "free election" pledges. MacLeish did bring up the view of "some writers" that the United States had given away too much on Poland. "To read them," said MacLeish in a manner that permitted little doubt about the preposterousness of the suggestion, "you'd think Poland had been sold down the river."

This gave Acheson an opportunity to defend the territorial settlement on the ground that very few ethnic Poles lived east of the Curzon line and the political settlement on the ground that there could be little quarrel with free elections. Congressman Alvin O'Konski replied on the House floor that Acheson's figures were false and were based on "misinformation" with "little regard for truth and justice." Senator Burton K. Wheeler offered similar criticisms.[110]

Acheson's exposition of the accords as simply the extraterritorial manifestation of public opinion involved a considerable amount of sophistry. In addition to the spreading disenchantment with the U.S.S.R. and, for that matter, with the British empire, public-opinion polls indicated the increased concern of some groups—Catholics, Polish-Americans, Jews—about events in Eastern Europe. No one was more sensitive to the votes wielded by these groups than Roosevelt, but the department chose to play up mass enthusiasm for the United Nations and to play down the doubts of particular groups within the attentive stratum of the public.

This gloss was not simply for public consumption. Even in private, State Department officers expressed satisfaction in the preponderant weight of mail to the department that approved the accords, overlooking the fact that most critical mail was sent to known supporters of the London Poles in Congress. Reports and memorandums typically included comments to the effect that "opposition has in general been from those habitually critical of the Administration's foreign policy," and could therefore be discounted.[111] Such judgments involved an element of self-delusion since many of the religious and ethnic groups most anxious about the Soviet Union were part of the New Deal coalition. [112] But a public-information campaign demanded "glittering generalities" rather than detailed attempts to discuss sources of friction in the postwar world.

Nonetheless, MacLeish had agreed, at Pasvolsky's prompting, to include a statement of the United Nations' limitations in the campaign. This can be seen in another theme of the radio series—the folly of "perfectionism." When a democracy embarks on educational or propaganda work it rapidly finds itself drawn into the denunciation of particular "isms" allegedly espoused by "some writers" or even "certain people." MacLeish and Under-Secretary Grew exchanged views on this subject in the program "Main Street and Dumbarton Oaks." The *practical* choice, according to Grew, was between an organization based on the Dumbarton Oaks proposals and "international anarchy." [113] The choice was not between the present proposals and "some ideal formula." This, MacLeish added was the position of the "perfectionists." The secretary himself warned against "perfectionism" in a speech in New York City on April 6. [114] "Perfectionism" was scarcely less pernicious than its polar opposite—"cynicism"—the view that any peacekeeping body was doomed to failure because war was rooted in human nature. The correct course, needless to say, was the narrow path between the two.

The last program in the radio series, "It's Your State Department," gave an account of the foreign service designed to dispel its image as a gilded anachronism that provided sinecures for graduates of Groton and Harvard. MacLeish claimed that not more than 1 percent of State's 9,580 employees had such an educational background. Salaries were modest; admission to the foreign service was by competitive examination, the result being "a pretty good cross section of the country's population." McDermott ridiculed the image of officers coming "to work at ten and knocking off for tea and cookies at four"; he described the long hours "commuting" to and from San Francisco to prepare press and radio coverage of the U.N. conference. MacLeish added: "We're lucky to get away at seven and luckier yet not to have to cart a briefcase of papers home to work on." And Assistant Secretary (formerly General) Holmes alleged that he would swap the department for a foxhole any day! [115]

This public-relations exercise was designed to build a public constituency for the kind of appropriations needed if the department were to reassert its hegemony. The department was depicted as a public advocate, a spokesman for the average American. This meant recasting foreign-policy objectives in terms of concrete, material interests. In the broadcast "It's Your State Department" MacLeish gave a classic exposition of the theory of a democratic foreign policy: "No foreign policy in a democracy is any better than the public support it receives and there can be no public support without public knowledge. The foreign policy of a democracy must reflect the people's will." Holmes completed the formulation: "If a foreign policy is not actively supported by the people it represents only the pious hopes of the officials who pull it out of the thin air." [116]

It is not surprising that the tribune of the people in this model should be none other than the Department of State: it canvassed, aggregated, articulated, and advocated the people's will. There was no scope for demagogy since the department would not step beyond the bounds scientifically indicated by its surveys of opinion. There was no scope for propaganda since democracy, self-determination, and the prevention of war were the common currency of all Americans. Within this framework, policy makers had only to find ways and means to realize the common aspiration.

The very operations that struck the administration's critics as manipulative and unworthy were living evidence of the American demos at work in foreign affairs: "Our information program here at home is a two-way proposition . . . . We study letters to the department very carefully . . . we also compile periodic summaries of what the press and radio are saying . . . and we study the public opinion polls with great care." These were matters of pride. Public opinion, Holmes conceded, "isn't the *only* consideration in formulating foreign policy. But it is one of the important things." MacLeish said it was vital. [117]

Not everyone agreed with the Department's apotheosis of public opinion. However the Division of Public Liaison was adept at pointing out that *most* of the comment was sympathetic and that negative comment, as usual, came from easily identifiable, habitual opponents of the administration. "One woman referred to the programs as the State Departments 'apologia pro vita sua' and indicated complete disbelief in the sincerity and intelligence of the Department." [118] Another correspondent thought the programs an unconstitutional abuse of the taxpayers' money.

Although the opinion analysts pointed out that no single criticism was supported by more than two of the handful of critical letters received, many of these themes were taken up in more influential circles. Congressman Taber, a congressional bane of OWI, took advantage of appropriation hearings to raise the perennial charge of abusing tax dollars to high pressure the public into supporting administration policies. A number of congressmen endorsed this general line. It was also adopted by organs of opinion that were unqualified opponents of Roosevelt and Truman, such as the *Chicago Tribune.* The *New York Herald Tribune* confined itself to criticism of technique, deploring the oversimplification of complicated problems.[119]

Despite this carping, analysts at State clearly perceived the radio series as an overall success. For MacLeish himself it represented a gratifying realization of hopes and plans that had been dashed by congressional and bureaucratic opposition in his days at OFF and OWI. For Dickey it represented the blossoming of an approach first tentatively applied in the 1930s. It confirmed Stettinius in his belief in the vital role of the modern media in public information work and encouraged him to continue to make extensive use of radio after the series ended.

ADVERTISING, PUBLICATIONS, AND PUBLIC SPEAKING

Early in January 1945, a proposal from the War Advertising Council to take advantage of its magazine outlets looked like a good opportunity to capture the imagination of the reading public: "The sooner we take advantage of this opportunity to tell our story," R. J. Lynch, special assistant to the secretary, wrote MacLeish, "the sooner we are going to successfully sell our objectives to the public." MacLeish and Stettinius agreed at once. They had to act decisively before the peace brought calls for retrenchment and further erosion of confidence in America's allies. All concerned were suffused with the lessons of 1919 and the 1930s. "They [the Advertising Council] feel that ninety million people represents a tremendous portion of our population, and if the story could be gotten over to these people, it would probably prevent the possibility of our becoming an isolationist country again as we did after the last war."[120] They planned to reach the people through 492 magazines in which space was available for patriotic purposes. They made extensive use of these facilities in succeeding weeks.

The department itself produced a series of pamphlets for mass distribution to individuals and groups on the theme "Building the Peace." The series presented the Dumbarton Oaks proposals, rather im-

moderately, as the potential solution for many of the world's most pressing problems: "War—How Can We Prevent It?" "Prosperity—How
Can We Promote It?" "Freedom—How Can We Achieve It?" With only
the faintest qualifications the answers were said to lie in the family of
U.N. agencies.[121] Here was the United Nations presented as the classic
expression of American liberalism.

From January to April the department's leading figures, as well as
officers from the foreign service, addressed professional associations and
opinion groups across the country. The same themes rang out, with the
notion of a "people's peace" being prominent.[122] This faintly recalled
Henry Wallace's "Century of the Common Man" address, which many
congressmen had found rather too sympathetic to America's great
Eastern ally. The entire effort culminated in April with a "Dumbarton
Oaks Week" on the eve of the San Francisco conference. It was run in
cooperation with many citizen groups that had been agitating for a collective security organization throughout the war.[123] In harmony with
the State Department's emphasis on a democratic decision the week
focused on an image of the United Nations as a town meeting of the
world. Town meetings in New England and an elaborately staged "town
meeting" in Carnegie Hall inNew York greeted their new senior partner.

ASSESSMENT

As the San Francisco conference convened State Department analysts
evaluated the impact of their unprecedented informational campaign.
"Awareness" of the Dumbarton Oaks proposals had undoubtedly increased during the campaign (see table 15). By March Cantril's organization reported that 73 percent of survey respondents had also heard of the
plans for the San Francisco conference, but many fewer were confident
of the conference's capacity to work out conditions for a durable
peace.[124] The publicity campaign obviously had not blanketed the
public with optimism on this score. Only 34 percent of those who had
heard of the impending conference thought that it would prevent world
war for the next fifty years; 26 percent thought that it would preserve
peace for the next twenty-five years. These figures need not be interpreted literally, but they do indicate something less than euphoria about
the prospects for keeping the peace.

TABLE 15
Have You Heard or Read of the Dumbarton Oaks Proposals?

	Yes	*No*
December 1944	43%	57%
February 1945	52	48
March 1945	60	40

Source: Public Attitudes on Foreign Policy, Department of State, May 11, 1945.

The information campaign had skirted problems with the U.S.S.R., preferring affirmations of the importance of maintaining unity and co-operation. Nonetheless, public distrust of the Soviet Union was on the rise. Successive revelations, of which the most recent was the relatively low-level delegation that the Soviets intended to send to San Francisco, led the public to question the U.S.S.R.'s commitment to the international security organization. When Acting Secretary Grew learned on March 24 that Ambassador Andrei Gromyko and not Foreign Minister Vyacheslav Molotov would head the Soviet delegation he sent an urgent memorandum to the president citing the probable impact on American opinion: "We feel that the absence of Mr. Molotov will have a very serious effect on public opinion and that the matter is of sufficient importance to warrant a message from you to Marshal Stalin." [125] Roosevelt's message failed to achieve the desired effect, leading to further speculation about public disenchantment and the possible cancellation of the conference. But on the day of Roosevelt's death Averell Harriman prevailed upon Stalin to relent, and it was agreed that Molotov would go to San Francisco via Washington. [126] His encounter with Truman in Washington has entered the annals of the cold war as the first sign of a decisive break between the Allies.

The information campaign had been less than candid about Soviet-American tensions just as Roosevelt, throughout the war, had taken few steps to alert the public to Stalin's known desiderata in Eastern Europe. No doubt the Polish-American vote contributed to his reticence in 1944. "The men in Washington feared adverse public reaction if the United States openly acknowledged the legitimacy of Russian ambition in Eastern Europe," Campbell comments. [127] But the real problem was not so much the admission of the "legitimacy" of such claims but rather the admission of the existence of serious rifts between the two allies. As late as May 26, 1945, MacLeish told the audience of an NBC broadcast that "the vital interests of the United States and the Soviet Union conflict at no point on the earth's surface." Both were "young, strong, self-confident countries," "independently rich in their own resources needing little from the world outside."[128] If there were differences, over Poland for example, they were insufficient to jeopardize continued collaboration.

Despite these troublesome areas, State Department analysts considered that the information campaign had been a success. On the eve of the conference they concluded that "a very general support of the Dumbarton Oaks proposals and of the San Francisco Conference exists in all sections of the country."[129] Robert Riggs demonstrates convincingly that the campaign did not arouse millennial expectations concerning the United Nations.[130] Our own examination confirms his view that the fourth point in the plan of campaign—the limitations of the United Nations—obtained adequate publicity. It was expressed in the disapproval of "perfectionism," in the insistence that great power unity was a necessary condition for the success of the organization, and in the restraint with which the ideal of world government was approached. Pasvolsky and others successfully intervened in the production of "Watchtower over Tomorrow" in order not to mislead the public into believing that the United Nations could be relied upon to take enforcement action when a dispute involved a permanent member of the Security Council.

But insistence on unity tended to displace analysis of the causes of disunity. It was in the nature of such a campaign, if not to foster euphoria, at least to accent the positive. The vision of a democratic decision to pursue collective security was a seductive one, which moved officials, including the secretary of state, to wishful predictions of a "peoples' peace." Such hopes contributed to a new current of internationalism in American public opinion, which policy makers were later to perceive as a fresh constraint when changes in the international system made collective security a less tenable instrument of high policy.

NOTES

1. Eisenhower to Early, August 2, 1943, *OWI Files*, National Archives, Federal Records Center, Suitland, Maryland.

2. Roosevelt to Hull, September 1, 1943, Elmer Davis Papers. Library of Congress.
3. Memorandum, Stettinius to the Secretary of State, November 1, 1943, Archibald MacLeish Papers, Box 847, Library of Congress.
4. Adam B. Ulam, *Expansion and Coexistence* (New York, 1968), p. 337.
5. See, for example, the references to Hull and the isolationists in Donald Watt, "Roosevelt and Neville Chamberlain: Two Appeasers," *International Journal* 28 (Spring 1973).
6. Richard J. Barnet, *Roots of War* (Baltimore, 1971), pp. 26-27. Wishing to bolster his case for an overweening military-industrial complex, Barnet denies that the State Department was ever to recoup its lost influence. Evidence in this and the next chapter challenges Barnet's contention. His stress on the persistence of military domination of the country's foreign policy after V-J day overlooks the fact that the war was followed by the largest demobilization in American history and a succession of immensely prestigious Secretaries of State. I am grateful to Stephen Adler for this observation.
7. Thomas M. Campbell, *Masquerade Peace: America's U.N. Policy, 1944-1945* (Tallahassee, Florida, 1973), p. 4.
8. Graham H. Stuart, *The Department of State* (New York, 1949), p. 382; Donald F. Drumond, "Cordell Hull," in Norman A. Graebner, ed., *An Uncertain Tradition: American Secretaries of State in the Twentieth Century* (New York, 1961), pp. 201-204.
9. Richard L. Walker, "E. R. Stettinius Jr.," in Robert H. Ferrell, ed., *The American Secretaries of State and Their Diplomacy* (New York, 1965), 14:10-12. It is of symbolical importance that one of Truman's early acts as president was to close down the White House map room and to restore State Department control over communications.
10. Morton H. Halperin and Arnold Kanter, *Readings in American Foreign Policy: A Bureaucratic Perspective* (Boston, 1973).
11. Harley F. Notter et al., *Postwar Foreign Policy Planning* (Washington, D.C., 1949).
12. Campbell, *Masquerade Peace*, p. 8.
13. Memorandum, "Observations and Suggestions on State Department Public Relations," Dickey to Assistant Secretary Howland Shaw, November 11, 1943, cited by Stuart, *Department of State*, p. 403.
14. Kenneth Colegrove, "The Role of Congress and Public Opinion in Formulating Foreign Policy," *American Political Science Review* 38 (October 1944).
15. *Department of State Bulletin* 11 (July 16, 1944).
16. Interview with John Sloan Dickey, April 17, 1973.
17. Its operating divisions were Division of Current Information; Division of Research and Publication; Motion Picture and Radio Division; Science, Education and Art Division; Central Translating Division. For details see Departmental Order 1218, *Department of State Bulletin* 10 (January 15, 1944).
18. In particular the furor over excessive "secrecy" at Dumbarton Oaks, discussed in the following section.
19. For a general study of the December reorganization, see Walter H. C. Laves and Francis O. Wilcox, "The State Department Continues Its Reorganization," *American Political Science Review* (April 1945).

20. Pasvolsky was also given authority over the Office of Special Political Affairs.
21. Dickey in Don K. Price, ed., *The Secretary of State* (Englewood Cliffs, 1960), p. 146.
22. MacLeish to Stettinius, December 9, 1944, Stettinius Papers, Box 224.
23. Ibid.
24. Stettinius to MacLeish, December 12, 1944, calendar note, Stettinius Papers, Box 224.
25. Calendar note, December 5, 1944, Stettinius Papers, Box 224.
26. *Chicago Tribune*, December 7, 1944.
27. Inis Claude, *Swords into Plowshares* (New York, 1964).
28. They were Joseph Grew for under secretary and, for assistant secretaries, Nelson Rockefeller, William Clayton, Julius Holmes, and James Dunn.
29. Calendar note, December 4, 1944, Stettinius Papers, Box 224.
30. *New York Times*, December 6, 1944.
31. Ibid., December 10, 1944.
32. Senate, Committee on Foreign Relations, *Nominations—Department of State* 78th Cong., 2d sess., December 12, 13, 1944.
33. Ibid.
34. *New York Times*, December 6, 1944.
35. Committee on Foreign Relations, *Nominations*, pp. 78-85.
36. Arthur M. Schlesinger Jr., *The Bitter Heritage: Vietnam and American Democracy* (Boston, 1966), p. 91; Ernest R. May, *"Lessons" of the Past: The Use and Misuse of History in American Foreign Policy* (New York, 1973), p. 179.
37. Memorandum for the President, May 13, 1944, Cordell Hull Papers, Box 65, File 285, Library of Congress. The memorandum also discussed the possibility of a constitutional amendment, which would modify the two-thirds rule for the ratification of treaties. This was considered and rejected, as a way to head off a possible Senate veto of the U.N. charter.
38. Dickey interview.
39. *Department of State Bulletin* (February 25, 1945): 288.
40. May, *"Lessons" of the Past*, p. 10.
41. Ibid., p. 12.
42. "Public Attitudes on Foreign Policy," Department of State, May 11, 1945.
43. *Peace and War: United States Foreign Policy, 1931-1941* (Washington, D.C., 1943), p. 3 and passim.
44. *Department of State Bulletin* (March 4, 1945): 357.
45. "That phrase did not come into circulation in the United States until 1934, but it fast gained currency with the rise of Germany, Italy and Japan as threats to the existing state of world affairs." Richard N. Current, "The United States and 'Collective Security': Notes on the History of an Idea," in Alexander DeConde, ed., *Isolation and Security* (Durham, North Carolina, 1957), p. 44.
46. Minutes, Political Subcommittee, January 30, 1943, MacLeish Papers, Box 40.
47. The second stage of the decision process outlined in chapter 1.
48. Minutes, Political Subcommittee, April 24, May 1, 1943. Leo Pasvolsky was general secretary of the subcommittee and Sumner Welles presided. Others present included MacLeish, Adolf Berle, Isiah Bowman, Senator Connally, and Harley Notter.
49. Ibid., April 24, 1943.

50. See, for example, Gabriel Kolko, *The Politics of War: The World and United States Foreign Policy, 1943-1945* (New York, 1968); David Horowitz, *The Free World Colossus: A Critique of American Foreign Policy in the Cold War*, rev. ed. (New York, 1971).

51. Minutes, Political Subcommittee, April 24, 1943.

52. William Appleman Williams, *The Tragedy of American Diplomacy* (New York, 1962), pp. 229-243.

53. In a covering note Cantril told Rosenman "We are not sending these results to anyone but you." However, the same analysis turns up in Stettinius's files, so the White House must have sent the report over to the State Department. The questions on which Cantril based the index are not recorded in his notebook. "The Wartime Notebooks of Hadley Cantril," vol. 4, Paper Center, Williams College.

54. The following is an example of these "leading" questions:

> If a candidate for President in 1944—either Democrat or Republican—made the following statements about what our policies should be after the war, which one would meet your greatest approval?
>
> We must give all necessary aid to friendly countries even at a good deal of sacrifice to ourselves. 31%
>
> We must not give so much aid to foreign countries that it will lower our standard of living here in this country. 64%
>
> No opinion. 5%

Ibid.

55. Ibid., vol. 4, Stettinius Papers, Box 394.

56. Minutes, Political Subcommittee, May 1, 1943, MacLeish Papers.

57. Robert A. Divine, *Second Chance: The Triumph of Internationalism in America During World War II* (New York, 1967).

58. "American Opinion Reports," May 11, 1945. These reports are located in files at the Office of Public Affairs, Department of State.

59. Jerome S. Bruner, *Mandate from the People* (New York, 1944), p. 45.

60. For a detailed discussion of the role of organized internationalist groups, see Divine, *Second Chance*.

61. Campbell, *Masquerade Peace*, p. 29.

62. Dickey interview.

63. *New York Times*, August 29, 1944.

64. Department of State, "American Opinion Reports," May 11, 1945.

65. On the agreement of Hull, Dewey, and Dulles to keep the subject of peace out of politics see the joint statement by Secretary Hull and Mr. Dulles, *Department of State Bulletin* 11 (August 27, 1944). See also the exchange of letters between Governor Dewey and Secretary Hull in ibid. (September 10, 1944).

66. Campbell, *Masquerade Peace*, pp. 65-66.

67. *New York Times*, August 23, 1944.

68. Dickey interview.
69. *New York Times*, November 21, 1944.
70. *Department of State Bulletin* 11 (October 22, 1944). The bulletin contains a list of organizations attending the meeting.
71. May, *"Lessons" of the Past*, p. 15.
72. Department of State, "American Opinion Reports," May 11, 1945.
73. Ibid.
74. Elihu Katz and Paul F. Lazarsfeld, *Personal Influence: The Part Played by People in the Flow of Mass Communications* (New York, 1955), pp. 309ff.
75. See for example the testimony of Henry Cabot Lodge to the House Subcommittee on International Organizations and Movements, 83d Congress, 1st sess., 1953, cited by Robert Riggs, "Overselling the U.N. Charter—Fact and Myth," *International Organization* (Spring 1960): 277. Reference to "overkill" from Dickey interview.
76. Ibid.
77. Department of State, "American Opinion Reports," May 11, 1945.
78. Ibid.
79. On the deterioration of relations between the big three in the months following Yalta, see John Lewis Gaddis, *The United States and the Origins of the Cold War, 1941-1947* (Columbia, 1972), and Diane Shaver Clemens, *Yalta* (New York, 1970), esp. pp. 265-291.
80. Secretary's Staff Committee minutes, February 6, 1944, Stettinius Papers, Box 396.
81. Ibid.
82. Ibid.
83. Ibid.
84. Secretary's Staff Committee minutes, February 10, 1945.
85. "Information Program with Respect to Dumbarton Oaks Proposals," Stettinius Papers, Box 396.
86. Campbell, *Masquerade Peace*, p. 6.
87. Stettinius Record, vol. 1, sec. 2, p. 21, Stettinius Papers, Box 245.
88. Secretary's Staff Committee minutes, May 30, 1945; Campbell, *Masquerade Peace*, p. 79.
89. Gaddis, *United States and the Origin of the Cold War*, p. 157.
90. Calendar note, December 8, 1944, Stettinius Papers, Box 224.
91. Ibid., December 18, 1944.
92. Ibid., December 27, 1944.
93. Ibid.
94. MacLeish to Harmon, December 29, 1944, Stettinius Papers.
95. Confidential memorandum, Foote to MacLeish, McDermott, and Dickey, January 13, 1945, Stettinius Papers, Box 220.
96. Ibid.
97. Foote to Stettinius, April 18, 1945, Stettinius Papers, Box 221.
98. Ibid.
99. Ibid.
100. Dickey, "The Secretary and the American Public," in Price, ed. *Secretary of State*, p. 147. Should any reader be moved to study the exhibit it can be found in the motion picture division of the Library of Congress.

101. Calendar note, December 27, 1944, Stettinius Papers, Box 224.
102. For a complete list of topics and dates, see *Department of State Bulletin* 12 (February 18, 1945).
103. Details of public reaction, size of audience, etc. are taken from "Public Reaction to Radio Broadcasts," prepared by the Public Attitudes Branch, Division of Public Liaison, Department of State, April 21, 1945, Stettinius Papers, Box 739. Radio scripts were printed in the *Bulletin*.
104. Department of State, "Public Response to the Report of the Crimea Conference," "American Opinion Report," March 6, 1945.
105. For detailed reaction to these developments see "American Opinion Reports," esp. those dated February 20, March 6, March 27, and April 24. Files may be consulted in the Office of Public Affairs, Department of State. Copies are also found in the Franklin D. Roosevelt Library, Stettinius Papers, and other manuscript collections.
106. *Department of State Bulletin* 12 (April 8, 1945).
107. Ibid. (February 25, 1945).
108. Ibid.
109. Ibid.
110. "Public Reaction."
111. Ibid.
112. May, *"Lessons" of the Past*, chap. 6.
113. *Department of State Bulletin* 12 (March 4, 1945).
114. Campbell, *Masquerade Peace*, p. 155.
115. *Department of State Bulletin* 12 (April 8, 1945).
116. Ibid.
117. Ibid.
118. "Public Reaction."
119. Mrs. Ogden Reid, publisher of the *New York Herald Tribune*, telephoned Stettinius to appologize for an editorial which wrote of "peace by propaganda." Calendar note, April 7, 1945, Stettinius Papers, Box 245.
120. Lynch to MacLeish. January 15, 1945, Stettinius Papers, Box 220.
121. *Department of State Bulletin* (April 1, 1945).
122. Remarks by MacLeish on "Information for a Peoples' Peace," *Department of State Bulletin* 12 (January 7, 1945).
123. Divine, *Second Chance*, pp. 284-285.
124. Department of State, "American Opinion Reports," May 11, 1945.
125. Grew to Roosevelt, March 24, 1945, President's Secretary's Files, Franklin D. Roosevelt Library.
126. Gaddis, *United States and the Origins of the Cold War*, pp. 200-201.
127. Campbell, *Masquerade Peace*, p. 141.
128. *Department of State Bulletin* 12 (May 27, 1945).
129. "Public Reaction."
130. Riggs, "Overselling the U.N. Charter."

5

A classic case of manipulation?

The final reorientation in American foreign policy that this study considers pinpoints the evolution of the opinion-policy relationship between the interwar and postwar periods. Truman's speech to the joint session of Congress on March 12, 1947, proposing economic and military assistance to Greece and Turkey has often been contrasted with Roosevelt's Chicago speech almost ten years earlier in which he proposed to quarantine the agressor nations. Many of Truman's listeners believed that it had been a fatal error not to heed Roosevelt's warnings; they were determined to profit from their earlier failure by giving an enthusiastic welcome to the "Truman Doctrine." The appeasement analogy was part of almost everyone's intellectual baggage in 1947, as congressional hearings and public debate on the Greek-Turkish aid proposals reveal.

It was an analogy shared, for example, by Under Secretary of State Dean Acheson and the "Second Secretary of State" Arthur Vandenberg, Republican chairman of the Senate Foreign Relations Committee. The senator wrote to a constituent that there was a "parallel" in the cleavage of the world between democracy and nazism in the 1930s and between democracy and communism in the 1940s. Of course, he wrote, "we shall never know whether history would have been different if we had all stood up to the aggressor at Munich. But at least we know what it cost to 'lie down.'" Referring to the Greek-Turkish aid proposal he added: "The adventure is worth trying as an alternative to another 'Munich' and perhaps to another war."[1]

If FDR's retreat from the quarantine speech has been treated as a classical case of a public-opinion constraint, the Truman Doctrine has been regarded as a classic example of the manipulation of public opinion to support a predetermined policy initiative. This interpretation of the relationship between public opinion and foreign policy in the 1947 case rests on three arguments: (1) that the definition of the situation as a *crisis* in American foreign relations sprang from domestic rather than international considerations; (2) that the presentation of the issues was designed to bring about a shift in public attitudes from reliance on collective security to acceptance of American responsibilities for maintaining security; (3) that the content as well as the style of the policy presentation was influenced, to a unique degree, by public-opinion specialists. "The question for modern controllers of American power," write Joyce Kolko and Gabriel Kolko, referring to the Truman Doctrine, "is not how to reflect the desires of the masses, but to manipulate them so that they endorse the needs and goals of men who might otherwise have to resort to sterner forms of repression to attain their ends."[2] The final clause reflects a position peculiar to certain neo-Marxist critics of American foreign policy but the rest of this analysis conforms with the view held by many moderate diplomatic historians.[3]

The Truman Doctrine has been treated exhaustively elsewhere as a turning point in the foreign relations of the United States.[4] Only the facet of this vast subject that casts light on the above interpretation will be considered here. Was this indeed a classic case of manipulation in which the public-affairs machinery created during and immediately after the war was employed to manipulate public sentiments? Or did those sentiments impinge on the formulation of policy?

DEFINITION OF THE SITUATION

On February 21, 1947, the British ambassador's private secretary delivered two notes to the State Department announcing that British aid to Greece and Turkey would be terminated in six weeks. The British government expressed the hope that the United States would take its place as the major source of foreign assistance to Greece and Turkey. This message created a situation of crisis for American decision makers, at least in the view of Acheson, Marshall, Truman, and their advisers. And, indeed, the situation fulfilled many of the criteria for the existence of a crisis that have been identified by political scientists. Charles Hermann, for example, points to "threat," "time," and "surprise" as conditions for the existence of a crisis. He elaborates: "A crisis is a situation that (1) threatens high priority goals of the decision making unit (2) restricts the amount of time available for response before the decision is transformed and (3) surprises the members of the decision making unit by its occurrence."[5]

The second of these criteria is the one most clearly satisfied by the delivery of the British message. British aid would end in six weeks. The United Nations Relief and Rehabilitation Agency (UNRRA) would also cease to function within that period. Failing any measures to provide substitutes, the prospect was for the collapse of the Greek economy and, it was assumed, its political independence. A Greek complaint to the Security Council spoke of foreign (i.e., communist) assistance to rebels in the north of the country. The situation in Turkey was less pressing. Its economic position was far stronger due in part to a profitable neutrality during the first five years of the war. It was not in a state of civil war or immediately threatened by outside pressures. The Soviet Union's claim to a share in the defense of the Dardanelles did not carry a deadline. The pressure of time was increased when Truman asked the Congress to decide on the Greek-Turkish aid bill within little more than a month.

Hermann's criterion of surprise was not satisfied by the British message. Both the severe condition of Britain's economy and its impending need for retrenchment in the Balkans were well known. Acheson and James Forrestal, secretary of the navy, had discussed the need to replace Britain as military and economic guarantor of Greece and Turkey the previous year.[6] Ever since the cessation of hostilities with Germany the Greek government had importuned Britain and the United States for economic aid. UNRRA served as a funnel for American assistance and, in January 1946, the Export-Import Bank agreed to a credit of $25 million for Greece. The mission under Paul A. Porter, sent by the State Department to study the situation in Greece, and the United Nations Food and Agriculture Organization had reported on the need for aid in reconstructing the Greek economy.

The description of Greek and Turkish conditions in the British notes came as no surprise to the State Department; this "we all knew," Dean

Acheson wrote in his memoirs.[7] Only the previous day, February 20, Acheson had worked up a paper for Marshall entitled "Crisis and Imminent Possibility of Collapse." The crisis in question was a Greek crisis, and the paper advocated substantial American aid. This need had been apparent through much of the previous year to high policy officers in the State, War, and Navy departments. Nonetheless, the imminence of the curtailment of British financial support crystallized the need for decision.

It is difficult to maintain that the information contained in the British notes "threatened high priority goals" of the United States since, hitherto, no such goals had been formulated or agreed to with respect to Greece and Turkey. Admittedly, the assurance of Western influence in the eastern Mediterranean formed part of Truman's general "get-tough" policy, the first signs of which appeared in 1945. British withdrawal presaged increased American influence in Greece, Turkey, Iran, and throughout the Middle East. But "toughness alone was not a policy." By the beginning of 1947 it was not clear what specific goals this policy enjoined "other than a disinclination towards further compromise with the Kremlin."[8] The British decision created the need to stop the drift in American foreign policy and to formulate those "high level goals," a threat to which is one of Hermann's conditions for the existence of a crisis situation. But there were not yet any *specific* high-level commitments that were threatened by the British notes. Without surprise or immediate threat to existing, high priority goals—even with the pressure of time—the situation in late February did not yet constitute a crisis in American foreign policy. In Hermann's typology the combination "high threat/short time/surprise" points to a crisis; the 1947 combination "low threat/short time/anticipated" rather suggests an "administrative situation."[9]

But the conditions for a crisis are found not only in the external situation. Howard H. Lentner interviewed a number of foreign service officers and high State Department personnel who had participated in "crisis management." On the basis of their responses he makes the following observation: "In addition to foreign policy goals—in the sense of American external relations with specific areas—decision makers in the Department of State pursue such goals as maintaining good relations with Congress, obtaining the support of the public, and providing effective service to the White House. Interviewees noted that a crisis can occur with respect to any of these goals."[10]

In the judgment of some of President Truman's contemporary critics it was congressional relations and the need for public support that generated the "crisis" in March 1947. Congressman George H. Bender of Ohio told his colleagues that the "Truman Administration is trying to steamroller [the assistance bill] through Congress with cries of 'crisis'" in order, he thought, to evade the objection that the proposals "by-passed the United Nations."[11] In his view the sense of crisis reflected internal political needs and pressures rather than those in the international system.

THE PUBLIC RESPONSE

The case for manipulation rests in large part on the argument that Truman and his advisers generated an *atmosphere* of crisis to elicit public and congressional support that might not otherwise have been assured. The external situation did not automatically *create* a situation of crisis for the United States. President Truman "could have decided that Greece was a country remote from the United States, with no immediate lines of communication; that it was far on the other end of the Mediterranean; that it was none of our business. He could have washed his hands of the whole thing or he could have done what he did."[12] This is no revisionist exegesis but the judgment of a seasoned practitioner, Charles Bohlen, who was close to General Marshall and alert to Soviet expansionism in 1947.

But Bohlen reduces the number of available choices by stating the alternatives in this way. Truman could have sought financial assistance, as in the case of the British loan, on the basis of local needs. A World War II ally that had fought fiercely against the German occupation was a good candidate for American assistance. Such a course had already been recommended by the U.N. Food and Agriculture Organization and by the American Porter mission. Nor need this have looked like another exasperating case of American altruism to members of the Congress. Will Clayton (assistant secretary of state for economic affairs) could present a powerful statement of the link between economic revival in Europe and American national interests. This link was especially strong where it concerned the periphery of the oil lands of the Middle East.[13]

However, information officers from the State, War, and Navy departments foresaw considerable opposition from Congress and the public.

The sources of opposition ranged from the most general—public apathy and the desire for a quite life—to the specific, for example, a preference for channeling aid through international institutions. By portraying the plight of Greece and Turkey as merely a facet of the general threat of totalitarian aggression, by evoking the already current appeasement analogy, the State Department hoped to keep wavering members of the bipartisan foreign-policy leadership in the fold. [14] The local Greek crisis would then become an American crisis in which vital national interests were at stake.

This part of the case for manipulation is by no means an ex post facto argument devised by revisionist historians. General Marshall himself was taken aback by the terms of Truman's request to the Congress for assistance to Greece and Turkey. The text reached him in Moscow as he was preparing for the conference of foreign ministers. "When we received the text," Bohlen, who was part of the American delegation, recalls:

> We were somewhat startled to see the extent to which the anti-communist element of this speech was stressed. Marshall sent back a message to President Truman questioning the wisdom of this presentation, saying that he thought that Truman was overstating the case a bit. The reply came back that from all his contacts with the Senate, it was clear that this was the only way in which the measure could be passed. [15]

Bohlen assumed that the sentiment that had to be overcome by this dramatic, ideological presentation was residual isolationism. Actually this was only a minor source of opposition among the mass public and in Congress. The speech and the accompanying information program were to neutralize other, more potent sources of doubt and uncertainty. These can be briefly summarized:

1. Depreciation of the communist threat to Greece and Turkey.
2. Dislike of aid to "reactionary" governments.
3. Residual isolationism.
4. Fear that the aid program would increase the likelihood of war.
5. Attachment to the United Nations and preference for handling the problem through international agencies.

The most salient of these themes in congressional hearings and floor debate was the fifth, followed by the second. Other criticisms were woven around these basic themes, notably dislike of seeming to shore up the British empire. Critics disparaged Truman's depiction of Greece and Turkey as protodemocracies, sometimes arguing that they were as totalitarian as the neighboring Soviet satellite states. Hostile members of Congress claimed that the public supported their criticisms and read George Gallup's public opinion reports, as well as reports from private constituency surveys, into the *Congressional Record*. The administration's principal supporters were ready to counter the introduction of such material by Burkean defenses of representative rather than plebiscitarian democracy. Members of Congress, Vandenberg thought, should make their own judgment about the competence of the United Nations and not be swayed by emotional, popular internationalism.

The congressional debate sparked by Truman's proposals was highly salient to the public. A National Opinion Research Center poll, dated April 3, 1947, found that 83 percent of a national sample had heard or read of congressional discussion of the president's proposals. This high level of familiarity was not accompanied by general agreement on the issues: disapproval of aspects of the Truman Doctrine ranged from 27 percent on the question of assisting Greece's economic recovery to 54 percent on the proposal to send military supplies to help Turkey. Table 16 summarizes the public's response to the three key aid proposals:

1. Do you approve or disapprove of our government providing money to Greece to help her recover from war?
2. Do you approve or disapprove of our sending military supplies to help the Greek governments?
3. Do you approve or disapprove of our sending military supplies to help Turkey?

Majority support for economic assistance to Greece was not carried over to military aspects of the program. Joseph Jones puts this down to the public's lack of "strategic realism," particularly with respect to the Soviet Union's plan to share with Turkey the defense of the Dardanelles.

There is no question concerning economic aid to Turkey since the $150 million in aid requested for that country was exclusively military. Of course military objectives did require certain logistical, civilian-type

TABLE 16
Truman Proposals

	Economic Assistance	Military Assistance	
	GREECE	GREECE	TURKEY
Approve	67%	37%	30%
Disapprove	27	53	54
No opinion	6	10	16

Source: National Opinion Research Center Survey, April 3, 1947.

projects such as road building. The difference in wording between questions 2 and 3 reflected the fact that Turkey was not in a state of civil war. The wording of question 1 is slightly misleading inasmuch as post-war recovery was only one of the purposes for which assistance to Greece had been requested. Truman clearly linked the economic with the political survival of Greece in his speech.

Economic aid for Greece was the least controversial item in the proposals and military assistance to Turkey the most controversial: 67 percent approval for the former sinks to 30 percent approval for the latter, while disapproval rises from 27 percent to 54 percent.

This response pattern was anticipated by the drafters of the March 12 speech. Jones and his colleagues considered that the American people were not yet accustomed to the kind of peacetime strategic military thought that underlay aid to Turkey. Also, it was predicted that Soviet propaganda would make the most of military build-ups on its periphery sponsored by the United States:[16]

It was therefore decided to play down military aid to Turkey and to present that aid, as could be done with truthfulness, in the context of Turkey's over-all economic situation. Military aid was not concealed but it was not emphasized.[17]

Reference to Turkey's overall economic position was disingenuous, for, unlike that of Greece, the Turkish economy was far from the brink of crisis. One senator, in his outrage at the attempt to gloss over the military character of American assistance to Turkey, even claimed that "the Turkish government is in the best financial condition in its history" because of war profiteering. [18] With press coverage of the congressional hearings, floor debate, and wider public discussion, the public could not long remain unaware of the military component of the plan.

According to an internal State Department public-opinion report, "popular concern for the U.N. was one of the central facts to emerge from the voluminous comment on the relation of this program [Greek-Turkish aid] to the U.N. The 'by-passing' of the U.N. was the common ground of criticism from the extreme left to the extreme right of those commenting." [19] The report was based on an analysis of elite and media opinion. But neither the State Department planners nor congressmen hesitated to impute a similar degree of internationalism to the mass public. In part this reflected a genuine understanding of the popular mood, as distilled by pollsters. In part, too, it reflected lingering attachment to the congressional conversion to collective security, which had been brought about in 1944 and 1945. The preference that pollsters were able to extract from the public for U.N. handling of the Balkan "crisis" in no way matched the intensity with which the issue was pursued in Congress. Indeed, among the mass public only the faintest association was visible between internationalism and opposition to the *economic* aspects of the proposals. [20] Yet the funneling of aid through international agencies, like the International Bank or the IMF, was a theme to which congressional opponents returned time and again. On another point— the repressive character of the Turkish regime and the shallowness of democracy in Greece—congressmen were also far more exercised than the mass public. Of course they were far better informed about conditions there as well.

Neither opponents nor friends of the aid bill doubted that "by-passing the U.N." was the most contentious aspect of the proposal. Here, for example, is the interpretation Senator Claude Pepper, a leading opponent of the bill, gave to an AIPO poll published on March 28, 1947, in the *Washington Post*: "The poll indicated that 56% of the people queried favored the bill asking for $250,000,000 to give aid to Greece, but the poll also indicated that a majority of the people regretted that we had not gone, in the first instance, through the United Nations organization, and the poll further disclosed that an overwhelming majority opposed our sending military missions to Turkey and to Greece." [21] Senator Pepper did not mention that polls also showed a high degree of attachment to the United Nations among those who *favored* Truman's program. No one questioned the preeminence of the "internationalist" source of opposition to the bill although its friends, such as Senator Vandenberg and James Reston of the *New York Times*, took the position that the issue was a spurious one because the United Nations was not equipped to handle the problem. [22]

The salience of the U.N. issue in the concerns of friends, as well as opponents, of the bill can be gauged from the words chosen by Senator Vandenberg, its chief sponsor, to introduce the measure on the Senate floor: "The Senate Foreign Relations Committee has unanimously reported the bill entitled 'A bill to provide assistance to Greece and Turkey.' It could be alternatively titled 'A bill to support the purposes of the United Nations to maintain international peace and security' or it could be titled 'A bill to serve America's self-interest in the maintenance of independent governments.'" [23] Never, it appeared, could an apparently explicit piece of legislation mean more things to more men. The need to neutralize opposition on the ground that the Truman Doctrine "by-passed" the United Nations had not been foreseen by the State Department. Indeed, the U.N. issue had scarcely been discussed at all in the State of War Navy Coordinating Committee (SWNCC) and State Department Planning sessions. This was surprising since the Office of Public Affairs had so recently been involved in an information campaign to mobilize support for the world body. Now the department was reaping its own dragon's harvest. Dean Acheson, Will Clayton, and other department witnesses devoted many long hours of congressional testimony to reasons why the United Nations could not be expected to take on the burden of Greece and Turkey.

Nothing could be more fatal to the United Nations, in Acheson's view, than to imbue it with qualities and strengths that it did not possess. Senators Albert Hawkes, Howard A. Smith, and Claude Pepper fired numerous questions at the acting secretary and his colleagues. Ought not Trygve Lie, the U.N. Secretary General, to have been informed? Ought not the United States to have solicited the opinions of the forty-nine U.N. members (out of a total of fifty-five) who usually voted with the United States? Acheson thought such solicitations inappropriate and unnecessary. They were ruled out, in any event, by the pressure of time imposed by a *crisis* situation.

It is most important that we should not, by attributing to the United Nations jurisdictions and powers and functions which it is either not designed to exercise or is not ready to exercise, inhibit ourselves and other states from performing very basic duties, which are necessary to maintain the underlying structure upon which the United Nations is based. [24]

But those who had been won over to the principle of collective security so recently, largely at the urging of the State Department, were not to be deflected lightly. Senator Pepper explored various proposals with Acheson for extending aid to Greece on a multilateral basis. One channel, he suggested, might be the United Nations Food and Agriculture Organization, which had recently recommended a reconstruction loan to Greece of $100 million. Another might be a new incarnation of UNRRA. Mayor La Guardia, the head of UNRRA, reported from Moscow that Stalin might consider contributing to UNRRA if it could be prolonged. Naturally this cut little ice with Acheson.

Pepper made the point that Greece's complaint about outside support for rebels in the north of the country was already before the Security Council. Might not the United States at least have waited for the report of the U.N. Commission of Enquiry before initiating unilateral action? Acheson could reply to this, with a lawyer's punctiliousness, that the proposed aid was *bi*lateral and not *uni*lateral since it was offered in response to Greek and Turkish requests. In addition he had a standby response, which depended on the administration's *definition of the situation*: multilateral agencies were appropriate for long-term assistance; decisive American action was needed in a *crisis*.

The sponsors of Senate bill 938 sought two routes of escape from these wrangles. Senator Vandenberg, chairman of the Foreign Relations Committee of the Senate since the Republican victory in the 1946 elections, proposed an "amendment," and former Senator Warren Austin, American delegate to the United Nations, took the government's case to the Security Council—sixteen days after Truman's speech. Shortly after these developments Francis Russell wrote: "I think it would not be too much to say in connection with the Greek crisis that force of public opinion had much to do with the recent speech by Mr. Austin before the UN and Senator Vandenberg's amendments." [25]

Vandenberg told the Senate, "I frankly regret that when the President spoke to Congress on March 12, he did not simultaneously advise the Secretary General at New York of our intentions, instead of waiting to present indirect notice through our representative on the Security Council sixteen days later."[26] Although there was a histrionic element in this demur at the timing of his State Department friends, the senator clearly spoke from conviction. He confided to his journal, "The Administration made a colossal blunder in ignoring the U.N.," [27] which he proposed to rectify with an amendment to the bill.

To Acheson this was pure Vandenberg but he was happy to go along with it. What amused Acheson was the senator's technique of finding a "minor" flaw in a piece of legislation, which, having once been corrected by a "Vandenberg Amendment," could be adopted by the Republican leadership without further qualms. "I lustily cried '*Peccavi*,'" Acheson contentedly recalls, "and offered to make amends. But the Senator was going to make the amends and the amendments himself."[28]

Vandenberg proposed a preamble to the bill, which rehearsed U.N. involvement in the Greek question to date, and an amendment that directed the president to suspend aid if the Security Council advised that it was no longer necessary because assistance had been forthcoming from international sources. According to Jones the Vandenberg amendment killed off any remaining opposition of any significance. [29] But the U.N. issue continued to be canvassed in the press and among internationalists in Congress. Senator Glen Taylor thought the amendment a transparent device to co-opt the opposition without making any substantial concessions to its views. "Confronted with the opposition of the American people to the by-passing of the United Nations," Taylor said in the Senate debate, "he [Vandenberg] sponsors an amendment which in its effect is no different from the old League reservations."[30] In other words it emasculated the world body by legitimizing the decision of great powers to act outside of it.

The second administration riposte to internationalist pressures was Warren Austin's tardy attempt to mend fences at the Security Council. This course was urgently pressed on the administration by a diverse group of individuals and organizations that had, so recently, been shepherded into the internationalist fold. The most ardent Republican proponent of the United Nations, John Foster Dulles, was in Moscow with General Marshall during the debate on the Truman Doctrine. But the Commission on a Just and Durable Peace of the Federal Council of Churches decided to proceed without waiting for the return of Dulles, its president. It issued a resolution generally endorsing emergency aid to Greece and Turkey, recognizing the threat posed by Soviet expansionism, but urging the government to seek the counsel and cooperation of the United Nations and to provide the Security Council with full information. [31]

Another little noticed group that was intensely distressed at Truman's failure to inform Trygve Lie of his impending proposals were the international civil servants and diplomats at Lake Success. U.N. Staff Morale Upset on Greece, read the headline of a *New York Times* story. [32] A nagging labor dispute about conditions for U.N. employees of various grades was exacerbated by Truman's speech. A survey of employees indicated that many believed the long-term prospects for their jobs had been diminished by the speech. "They are asking if the United Nations was not established to handle precisely that kind of a problem, then why was it established? This, of course, has a direct relationship with their own status and morale." [33] A poll of diplomats from thirty-two countries at the United Nations, published in May, revealed that 82 percent thought the Truman policy hurt the prestige of the United Nations. [34]

Austin's speech was conciliatory in tone and did not dwell on the chasm between totalitarianism and democracy. He reaffirmed America's support for the principle of collective security and expressed the hope that in the future international bodies would assume more responsibility in Greece. Like Acheson's testimony and Vandenberg's presentation of his amendment, Austin's justification for unilateral American action rested on a definition of the situation in terms of crisis. He distinguished between long-term and emergency measures. The United Nations was in the process of equipping itself for the former; the United States had stepped into the breach to provide *emergency* assistance: "It is by combining national and international action of both immediate and long-range character and aimed both at the security and economic aspects of the problem that the members of the United Nations can advance the cause of collective security." [35] He expressed the hope that, in the future, the Economic and Social Council of the Economic Commission for Europe would interest itself in the problems of Greece. This was an additional reason for the rapid establishment of that body. Rather ingeniously he argued that emergency American aid would make Greece a better risk for loans from the International Bank in the future.

In keeping with postwar concepts of a democratic American foreign policy, explored in chapter 4, Austin acknowledged public agitation about bypassing the United Nations and referred to the "intensity of our democratic debate and the keen desire of our people to see the United

Nations grow in authority and confidence."[36] They were anxiously awaiting the report of the Security Council's Commission of Enquiry. Meanwhile the economic assistance Truman proposed was congruent with the FAO recommendation that Greece seek aid from Britain and the United States. Thus he endeavored to show that the Truman Doctrine did not detract from American commitment to collective security.

To ardent internationalists it seemed that, like the good soldier Svejk, the United States was giving a nod to established authority while resolutely marching in the opposite direction.[37] From the perspective of the 1970s the wonder is not that the United States marched to the defense of Greece and Turkey but that it gave such an emphatic nod to the United Nations. To be sure, President Kennedy placed considerable importance on a plausible presentation of the American position to the United Nations during the Cuban missile crisis. But, by 1962, the principle of "selective" security action by the superpowers was an established precedent. In 1947 the American government still felt itself to be somewhat hedged in by the popular bipartisan enthusiasm for the United Nations that it had done so much to foster in 1944 and 1945.

The possibility of such enthusiasm constituting a constraint on America's freedom of action had been foreseen by a few State Department "realists" who had tried to prevent the United Nations from being oversold. In formulating the information campaign boosting the Dumbarton Oaks proposals and the charter Pasvolsky had stressed U.N. limitations with respect to enforcement actions where the great powers were involved. In 1947 additional limitations were visible in the incapacity of multilateral agencies to provide speedy economic assistance. Although Acheson and Austin liked to state the problem in terms of the *mechanics* of such aid, the fact was that this situation potentially meant confrontation between the United States and the Soviet Union.

In a secret memorandum prepared for Pasvolsky's consideration at the end of 1944 R. W. Hartley made some Cassandra-like predictions. The memorandum acknowledged the immediate need to build up public pressure for American support of collective security.[38] But, in the longer run, he warned, "The tide in public opinion, once created upon this basis, will run so strong that it will probably hamper—in a sense—the flexible features of an 'ideal' American foreign policy. Ideally an international organization should be only the 'first line of defense' in the security considerations of our foreign policy. However, to admit publicly such a consideration would tend to cast doubt in the popular mind on the more basic premise, i.e. that an international organization is, in the end, the most effective and economical way to maintain American security."[39]

Hartley correctly foresaw that at some future time America's desire to pursue some major line in foreign policy *outside* the United Nations might run into opposition from internationalists whose enthusiasm had been needed to carry the United States into the organization. But in keeping with the lessons of the past that were drawn in 1944, he mistakenly predicted that unilateral moves outside the United Nations would lead the public back to Fortress America. He had not anticipated that the relegation of collective security to a position as the second line of defense would be accompanied by a new doctrine that provided for a forward American position in world affairs.

Contemporary press reports during the House and Senate debates, coupled with AIPO, NORC, State Department, and Princeton polls, indicated that part of Hartley's prediction had been realized. Despite the exertions of realists during the earlier promotion of the United Nations, "One of the troubles with the United Nations today is that it has been oversold," according to a *Washington Evening Star* report read into the *Congressional Record* by Congressman Keating. It continued:

> Through the medium of loose statements many people have acquired a grossly exaggerated notion of the contribution of peace and security which the organization is capable of making at this time. The danger of this is that when the truth becomes generally known there will be cynical reaction in this country which will seriously undermine American support for the UN.[40]

Chapter 4 indicated that the United Nations had not been oversold inasmuch as the information campaign included warnings of limitations as well as possibilities. But the limitations sounded rather like technical quibbles in a presentation that was overwhelmingly positive. Now, in 1947, stress on the limitations was the new orthodoxy.

Because the administration laid so much emphasis on public endorsement of the Truman Doctrine, a point Austin hammered home at Lake Success, senatorial opponents of the message themselves frequently cited the opinion polls. Both Pepper and Taylor came back time and again to Gallup figures published in the *Washington Post* on March 28 and April

13 (see table 17). They were both struck by the fact that the impact of the public debate on American opinion had been to *increase* the percentage believing that the problem of aid to Greece and Turkey should be turned over to the United Nations. Other senators and congressmen read into the *Record* the results of private constituency polls, all of which pointed to disapproval of the Truman proposals unless handled through the United Nations. Senator Pepper drew from these the conclusion that "the American people have not been so troubled by anything since the end of the war as they are by the bypassing of the United Nations in the making of this decision by the government of the United States."[41]

TABLE 17

Do You Think the Problem of Aid to Greece and Turkey Should Be Turned over to the United Nations?

	Yes	No	Don't Know
March 28, 1947	56%	25%	19%
April 13, 1947	63	23	14

Source: Congressional Record, April 17, 1947, p. 3591. Dates refer to publication of report.

Appeals to the American demos brought rejoinders from sponsors of the bill on both theoretical and practical grounds. Senator Taylor asked the chairman of the Foreign Relations Committee "whether his amendments carry out the philosophy and wish of the people, as expressed in these polls." He raised the question because Gallup had said that the Vandenberg amendment satisfied the popular demand for a "nod" toward the United Nation. Senator Vandenberg gave a classically Burkean rejoinder to the plebiscitarian argument implicit in Senator Taylor's frequent readings from Gallup:

Although I have always found the Gallup poll interesting and encouraging when it agreed with my point of view, I have not formed the habit of considering the Gallup poll to be in the same classification as either the Constitution or the Bible. This is not a pure democracy in which we live where Gallup polls are the controlling consideration. I quite agree that insofar as they reflect public opinion accurately—and frequently they apparently do—they are of very great interest to a representative body of this character ... but I would hardly be able to rest my opinion in respect to a problem of this fundamental importance upon a Gallup poll. [42]

In addition to these considerations of representative democracy, Vandenberg thought that since senators themselves were so poorly informed on the situation in Greece and Turkey, even after weeks of debate, the probability that Gallup had succeeded in contacting individuals who were better informed was rather low. This, of course, overlooked the fact that polls contain information about opinions rather than information about strategic and economic conditions abroad.

However fascinating an insight these disquisitions provide on contemporary understandings of the opinion-policy relationship, the real answer to the charge that the Truman Doctrine "by-passed the United Nations" lay elsewhere, for the special pleading of Acheson, Vandenberg, and other proponents of the bill was rooted in reality. There was no U.N. military staff committee, there was no U.N. international reconstruction fund capable of taking the place of UNRRA; the International Bank was just getting organized and the International Monetary Fund was not permitted to make loans without the reasonable expectation of their being repaid within the foreseeable future. Pasvolsky had injected into the 1944-1945 information campaign the proviso that the effectiveness of the United Nations depended on great power unity, and, of course, this condition had not been satisfied. Some conservative congressmen reached the conclusion by March 1947 that the Soviet Union had not joined the United Nations in good faith, as witnessed by its refusal to participate in a host of U.N. agencies designed to promote better understanding. [43] The United Nations was a red herring in terms of the realities of international relations, although it remained a potent source of domestic dissent.

Considerably less salient but nonetheless prominent in congressional criticism was "dislike of aid to reactionary governments." This theme was far more significant in elite than in mass opinion, no doubt because the opinion leadership was much better informed about conditions in Greece and Turkey. This did not prevent congressmen from giving way to hyperbole in their condemnation of the repressive character of their regimes.

Criticism on this score had been predicted by Francis Russell, chairman of the SWNCC Subcommittee on Foreign Policy Information, which monitored the campaign boosting Truman's proposals. In a strategy session on February 28 he pointed out that "the question would be raised about US plans to support the monarchy" in Greece. [44] This he thought would offend Republican sensibilities even without the question of repression. The view that congressional opposition would latch on to the fact that Greece was a monarchy was accurate as far as it went. But Senator Taylor, Helen Gahagan Douglas, and others had more searing political and economic grievances. Taylor quoted from a UNRRA report that described Greek economic conditions, maldistribution of income, the burden of taxes on the poor, and so on. He was equally appalled by political repression. "In Greece at the present time there is a Nazi-type dictatorship which we propose to aid," he said in a Senate speech. [45]

John Jernegan, who represented State on the SWNCC subcommittee, "thought that [we] should stress the fact that Greece is a constitutional monarchy, exercising very little power." [46] He thought the information campaign should also broadcast the fact that British and American observers were present at the recent Greek elections. The Greek people had agreed, by plebiscite, to retain the monarchy, and measures of reform were underway. Despite all this he agreed, "It is true the government is corrupt, but it is not basically fascist. Ought to make that point clear to counteract leftist propaganda." [47] Russell thought neutralization of this line of attack so important that he moved it to the position of "Item 1" on the agenda of the information program. [48]

Very little attention was devoted to Turkey in the program. Jernegan reminded the subcommittee that it should not forget about Turkey but Llewelyn Thomson said that it should not be emphasized in the information program. He saw the Turkish issue arousing fears of war since virtually all aid for Turkey was military. [49] "Military aid to Turkey was not concealed but it was not emphasized," writes Jones with a touch of glee at an adroit maneuver in a just cause.

In addition to the fear of war an equally pressing reason for softpedaling Turkey was the nondemocratic character of its regime. Turkey lacked the associations with democracy that the Western mind links to Greece, regardless of lapses. Numerous press reports were inserted in the *Congressional Record* describing the harassment of opposition figures in Turkey and the weight of censorship. For both realistic geopolitical reasons and because most palpably Turkey was not a democracy, aid to Turkey had to be played down and couched in strategic military terms.

"If the communists succeed in seizing control in Greece," the SWNCC

scenario ran, "Turkey will be threatened because of the strategic position of the Greek mainland and Greek islands and consequently the
whole Near East."[50] Congressmen were to be reminded not only of the
political costs of appeasement but of the tangible assets in material
resources, particularly oil, that lay in the Soviet Union's path between
Ankara, Azerbaidzhan, and the Persian Gulf. The best comment on the
information strategy of playing down Turkey was provided by a witness
before the House Committee on Foreign Affairs who said, noting the
virtual absence of comment on Turkey volunteered by the bill's sponsors,
"When the bill was being prepared for American consumption, Turkey
was slipped into the oven with Greece because that seemed to be the
surest way of cooking a tough bird."[51]

But this piece of prestidigitation did not escape congressional notice.
After all, $150 million of the total request for $400 million was ear-
marked for Turkey. "It is often forgotten," Senator Taylor said, "that
half the President's proposal is concerned with Turkey. Turkey has abso-
lutely no relief needs. During the war it enjoyed a long, lush uninter-
rupted war boom. It sold supplies to both sides and both sides paid and
paid very well. The only purpose of aid for Turkey is a military one." This
had been conceded already though clouded by Acheson's references to
the "constitutional" character of the regime[52] and the generally
Manichean terms of the administration's presentation.

As in the U.N. information campaigns of 1944 and 1945, a basic decision to stick to a realistic account of the issues was swayed by the desire to
appeal to the strains of idealism in the target audience. Such a desire
flowed more from conviction than from cynicism. But beneath the rheto-
ric of Taylor, Pepper, and Johnson, who knew how to match the administration in hyperbole, there was an element of intellectual toughness that
refused to put a gloss on the absence of political liberties in countries that
the United States had decided to support for other reasons. "By no stretch
of the imagination can Turkey be said to be on the road to democracy,"
declared Senator Johnson of Colorado, "even though our State Department gracefully approves the brutal, harsh and ruthless dictatorship that
controls that nation. The Senate ought to be more realistic. Military aid
and assistance to this government is aid and assistance to a Fascist military dictatorship."[53] Helen Gahagan Douglas was in the forefront of
those offering similar criticisms in the House. The cavalier use of the
terms "fascist," "Nazi," and "totalitarian" can no more be excused in
the case of critics than it can in the government's case. But beneath the

loose language was the same kind of outrage that had burned in General Stilwell when mendacious reports of Chiang Kai-shek's achievements and prospects circulated in Washington. Throughout the cold war, which, in a sense, became official with the March 12 speech, critics of American foreign policy railed against self-deception concerning non-democratic regimes that the United States has supported.

The Senate's cherished right of unrestricted debate, even under the "crisis" conditions of March and April 1947, and the fact that the House considered the bill after the Senate, allowed for a prolonged airing of these criticisms in the legislature and, hence, in the press. But they were peripheral in the minds of most congressmen and should not be got out of proportion. The bill was never in serious jeopardy. Once this fact was grasped even its supporters could afford to indulge the grievances of their colleagues who took a sterner view. In any event, the legislation passed the Senate by a large bipartisan majority of 67 to 23 on April 22 and the House by an equally impressive margin of 287 to 107 on May 9.

THE CASE FOR MANIPULATION: ASSESSMENT

Did this result indicate that the administration had successfully "manipulated" public opinion? It will be recalled that the case for manipulation is based on three arguments:

1. That the definition of the situation in terms of a "crisis" in American foreign relations sprang from domestic rather than international considerations.

2. That the presentation of the issues was designed to induce a shift in public attitudes from reliance on collective security to acceptance of American responsibilities for maintaining security.

3. That the content as well as the style of the new policy was influenced to an extraordinary degree by the advice of public-opinion specialists.

The first argument for manipulation rests on the definition of the situation made by those who drafted the March 12 speech and prepared the accompanying "educational" campaign. The evidence considered here shows that, faced with an indifferent public and a stipulation from Vandenberg and Connally that the administration make a bold and persuasive statement of the issues, the government generated an atmosphere of "crisis" that external events alone did not warrant. The decision to portray the situation in terms of a global clash of ideologies was a response both to Soviet expansionism and to the need to mobilize domestic consent. It was not a cynical decision. Even Richard Barnet, a proponent of the "manipulation" thesis, writes, "In fairness to Acheson it must be said that he and the other top managers of the American foreign policy did believe in the threat of a monolithic world communism."[54] No one who has read the minutes of the SWNCC subcommittee strategy sessions, or even Joseph Jones's published account of the drafting of the speech, can doubt that beneath the public relations angling lay a profound conviction of the threat Soviet expansionism posed. But it was the anticipation of domestic opposition that transformed a general threat into a living "crisis."

Ernest May reminds us how much scope the president has to determine the proportion of external events: "Presidents have made much or little of an event and thus determined its importance for Congress and the public."[55] John Kennedy might have shrugged off the installation of missiles in Cuba as Secretary Robert MacNamara was at first inclined to do; Nixon might have raised the alarm about the extension of Soviet naval power in the Mediterranean.[56] Truman "could have decided that Greece was a country remote from the United States . . . ; that it was far on the other end of the Mediterranean; that it was none of our business."[57] But he chose to define the situation as an American crisis—in part because of the ubiquitous acceptance of the appeasement analogy, in part because of the need to persuade doubters close to home.

The second part of the case for manipulation consists in the argument that the March 12 speech and accompanying promotional campaign induced a shift in popular beliefs, notably in attitudes towards the U.S.S.R.

Popular distrust of the U.S.S.R. had been growing ever since the "false dawn" of postwar amity at Yalta. This distrust fed into the policy process—via the Office of Public Affairs' Public Studies Division—and was regularly transmitted by Russell to higher officers.[58] No doubt popular sentiments contributed to the stiffening of American policy toward the Soviet Union, but the flow of influence was not unidirectional. The information in table 18 indicates that distrust of the Soviet Union jumped by seventeen points between December 1946 and March 1947. The March poll was taken after the president's speech.

TABLE 18

Do You Think Russia Can Be Trusted to Cooperate with Us?

	Yes	No	Don't Know
September 1945	52%	33%	15%
October 1945	40	44	16
March 1946	34	45	21
June 1946	30	55	15
October 1946	28	58	14
December 1946	35	46	19
March 1947	25	63	12

Source: Department of State, "American Opinion Reports," April 11, 1947.

In dispatching this data to his chief, Assistant Secretary Benton, Russell commented that "the Greek-Turkish crisis did increase, apparently, public 'distrust' of Russia."[59] But there had been no international events of the magnitude of Hitler's claim to the Sudetenland or even the Azerbaidzhan affair during the preceding six months. So Russell's observation that there was a "considerable correlation between events on the international scene and public attitudes toward Russia" did not apply in early 1947. Otherwise it has been well borne out by subsequent research.[60]

Not all who were distrustful of the U.S.S.R. approved of President Truman or his doctrine. Distrust of the Soviet Union *and* of Truman's program were compatible with general disapproval of a strong and active American role in world affairs. But comparatively few Americans reacted to the latest incarnation of totalitarianism by proposing a retreat to isolationism.

Another shift in popular sentiments that pollsters attributed to the announcement of the Greek-Turkish aid program concerned President Truman's personal popularity. Public approval of his "handling of his job" increased sharply from 48 percent in February 1947 to 60 percent in March, following the speech. The Roper poll also suggested that Truman's performance in the "crisis" had increased his presidential stature.[61] These figures support the contention that the attraction of Greece and Turkey for Truman lay in the opportunity they provided for him to demonstrate strong leadership.[62] Seeing little scope for dramatic innovation on the home front, with a Republican Congress, the president viewed foreign policy as the realm within which he might best establish his authority.

The third argument for manipulation addresses the mode of policy formulation after the delivery of the British notes. The Truman Doctrine is, perhaps, unique in major American foreign policy initiatives in that much of its content was determined by information rather than policy officials. By 1947 the Office of Public Affairs and the Foreign Policy Information Subcommittee of SWNCC had acquired so much prestige that a new policy was almost synonymous with a new information program. The March 12 speech, George Kennan later wrote,

> had been produced at the initiative of the [State] Department's public relations office, in a subcommittee of the State-War-Navy Coordinating Committee [SWNCC] which evidently felt itself under the necessity of clothing the announced rationale for the President's decision in terms more grandiose and more sweeping than anything that I, at least, had ever envisaged. [63]

Needless to say Kennan is not an impartial witness; he nourished a growing resentment at the misconstruction of the policy of containment, which he had earlier propounded.

Another scarcely less engagé witness, Joseph Jones, remembers that "policy-operations officers were among the most effective in making suggestions on the tone and content of the public approach and the information officers were equally effective in analyzing strategic and political considerations."[64] Jones was naturally gleeful at succeeding to the policy role that had eluded high information officers, among them MacLeish, through the bureaucratic history of OFF, OWI, and the State Department. His account is highly subjective and tends to exaggerate the role of Joseph Jones, who is always referred to in the third person. But it is undeniable that many of the critical points in the Truman Doctrine were taken verbatim from conversations among information officers and drafts they produced. The portrayal of the local situation in the Balkans as part of an epic, global struggle had its genesis in their perceptions, or misperceptions, of probable domestic opposition.

These arguments for "manipulation" are scarcely conclusive, or rather, the demonstration of successful "manipulation" does not imply that the public had no influence. Why was manipulation necessary at all if policy makers did not feel constrained by public and congressional opinion? "The question before the Truman administration," write the Kolkos, two of the principal proponents of the manipulation view, "was not how to reflect public opinion, or even to change it, but how to overcome its potentially negative consequences."[65] This reveals circular reasoning at the heart of the manipulation argument; for, if policy makers had to overcome the potentially negative consequences of public opinion they were not immune to it. The clearest example of a modification of the official position as a result of public pressures after the speech was Acheson's acceptance of the Vandenberg amendment. "Force of public opinion had much to do with the recent speech by Mr. Austin before the U.N. and Senator Vandenberg's amendments," Russell wrote.[66] He recalls that Acheson and his colleagues paid close attention to the polls during debate over the bill.[67] Perhaps this was a trivial modification in policy. But at the time it seemed like an important concession to popular internationalism, and it created a precedent that led presidents in other "crises" at least to present the issues to the United Nations.

"The potentially negative consequences" of public opinion were also weighed in the definition of the situation. There is nothing sinister or even unusual about a crisis arising from an interplay between domestic and international events.[68] The congressional leadership itself was unmoved by Marshall's dry recitation of the plight of those distant lands. Only Acheson's highly charged restatement of the situation in global, ideological terms lit a spark among the opinion leadership. It was natural to expect that the mass public would remain unmoved by anything less than a clear and present danger to American national interests—all the more so since, in Jones's words, the public was uncritically sold on the United Nations. Only a rousing appeal could undo the work of previous information campaigns and of postwar lassitude. Neither congressional fears about the failure of the bill and an electoral backlash nor administration perceptions of popular sentiment necessarily reflected reality. Public judgments were based on ignorance concerning conditions in the Balkans, and congressional opposition was vocal but peripheral in voting strength. Advance knowledge of success could not have been the lot of those who contemplated a bold and, in contemporary terms, revolutionary shift in American foreign policy.[69] A slight exaggeration of the dangers to the United States and of the imminence of crisis was a small price to pay for the mobilization of public consent.

NOTES

1. Letter dated May 12, 1947 in Arthur H. Vandenberg, Jr., ed., *The Private Papers of Senator Vandenberg* (Boston, 1952), p. 342.
2. Joyce Kolko and Gabriel Kolko, *The Limits of Power: The World and United States Foreign Policy, 1945-1954* (New York, 1972), p. 334.
3. E.g., Charles E. Bohlen, *The Transformation of American Foreign Policy* (New York, 1969), p. 87; John Lewis Gaddis, *The United States and the Origins of the Cold War, 1941-1945* (New York, 1972).
4. E.g., Department of State, *Foreign Relations of The United States, 1947* (Washington D.C., 1972); Dean Acheson, *Present at the Creation: My Years in the State Department* (New York, 1969); Stephen E. Ambrose, *Rise to Globalism: American Foreign Policy, 1938-1970* (Baltimore, 1971); Lloyd C. Gardner, *Architects of Illusion: Men and Ideas in American Foreign Policy 1941-1949* (Chicago, 1970); Louis J. Halle, *The Cold War as History* (New York, 1967); Kolko and Kolko, *Limits of Power*; Joseph M. Jones, *The Fifteen Weeks* (New York, 1955); George F. Kennan, *Memoirs*, vol. I: *1925-1950* (Boston, 1967); William A. Williams, *The Tragedy of American Diplomacy* (New York, 1959); Ernest R. May, *"Lessons" of the Past: The Use and Misuse of History in American Foreign Policy* (New York, 1973); Andre Fontaine, *History of the Cold War* (New York, 1968), vol. 1.
5. Charles F. Hermann, "Some Issues in the Study of International Crisis," in Hermann, ed., *International Crisis: Insights from Behavioral Research* (New York, 1972), p. 13.
6. Walter Millis, ed., *The Forrestal Diaries* (New York, 1951), p. 2.
7. Acheson, *Present at the Creation*, p. 217.
8. Richard D. Burns, "James F. Byrnes," in Norman A. Graebner, ed., *An Uncertain Tradition: American Secretaries of State in the Twentieth Century* (New York, 1961), p. 243.
9. Hermann's typology of situations includes eight permutations of these three dimensions ranging from "crisis" to "administrative" situations. Hermann, *International Crisis*, p. 14.
10. Howard H. Lentner, "The Concept of Crisis as Viewed by the United States Department of State," in ibid., p. 117.
11. *Congressional Record*, 80th Cong., 1st sess., p. 4692.
12. Bohlen, *Transformation of American Foreign Policy*, p. 86.
13. Gardner, *Architects of Illusion*, pp. 113-138; Senate, Committee on Foreign Relations, *Hearings on a Bill to Provide for Assistance to Greece and Turkey*, 1st sess., 1947, pp. 63-91 (hereafter *Senate Hearings*).
14. Memorandum, "Information Program on U.S. Aid to Greece," n.d., drafts of Truman Doctrine folder, Joseph M. Jones Papers, Harry S. Truman Library.
15. Bohlen, *Transformation of American Foreign Policy*, p. 87.
16. SWNCC, Subcommittee on Foreign Policy Information Meeting, February 28, 1947, "Important Relevant Papers" folder, Jones Papers. Jones, *Fifteen Weeks*, p. 162.
17. Jones, *Fifteen Weeks*, p. 162.
18. Senator Johnson of Colorado, *Congressional Record*, p. 3293. All references to the *Congressional Record* in this chapter refer to the 80th Cong., 1st sess., unless otherwise stated.

19. Department of State, "American Opinion Reports," December 27, 1948. These reports are located in files at the Office of Public Affairs, Department of State.

20. Survey Research Center, University of Michigan, *Public Attitudes Towards American Foreign Policy* (Ann Arbor, 1947), pt. 1.

21. *Congressional Record*, p. 3281.

22. *New York Times*, March 18, 1947.

23. *Congressional Record*, p. 3195.

24. *Senate Hearings*, p. 48.

25. Memorandum, Russell to Benton, Department of State, April 11, 1947, Office of Public Affairs files.

26. *Congressional Record*, p. 3198.

27. Vandenberg Papers, p. 345.

28. Acheson, *Present at the Creation*, p. 224.

29. Jones, *Fifteen Weeks*, p. 184.

30. *Congressional Record*, p. 3403.

31. *New York Times*, March 26, 1947.

32. Ibid., March 16, 1947.

33. Ibid.

34. Poll conducted by the United Nations *World Magazine*. Results read into *Congressional Record* by Congressman Bender of Ohio, May 7, 1947. *Congressional Record*, p. 4692.

35. *New York Times*, March 29, 1947.

36. Ibid.

37. Senator Taylor referred to a Gallup report that appeared in the *Washington Post*, March 28, 1947, under the headline Nod to un Popular.

38. Memorandum, "United States Foreign Policy and the International Organization," December 19, 1944, Papers of Leo Pasvolsky, Library of Congress.

39. Ibid.

40. *Washington Star News*, March 27, 1947; *Congressional Record*, p. 4807.

41. *Congressional Record*, p. 3287.

42. Ibid., p. 3490.

43. Congressman Richards of South Carolina made the point that the U.S.S.R. had failed to join UNESCO, the World Bank, the IMF, the FAO, the International Civil Aeronautic Organization, the ILO, the WHO, and the International Refugee Organization. Ibid., p. 4690.

44. The Foreign Policy Information Subcommittee of SWNCC was the main body to devise and monitor the public presentation of the Truman Doctrine. The mechanics of the information program have not been reproduced in this chapter. They can be followed in detail in the memorandums in n. 14 and n. 16 above. Jones draws heavily on these for his published account in *Fifteen Weeks*. The information program can also be read in outline in Manfred Landecker, *The President and Public Opinion* (Washington D.C., 1968), pp. 94-95. The use of the media, background briefings, and so on followed the precedent and practice of the 1944 and 1945 campaigns for the United Nations.

45. *Congressional Record*, p. 3394.

46. See n. 16 above.

47. Ibid.

48. Ibid.
49. Ibid.
50. See n. 14 above.
51. Jones, *Fifteen Weeks*, p. 163.
52. *Senate Hearings*, p. 24.
53. *Congressional Record*, p. 3294.
54. Richard J. Barnet, *Roots of War: The Men and Institutions behind US Foreign Policy* (Baltimore, 1971), p. 274.
55. May, *"Lessons" of the Past*, p. 153.
56. Ibid.
57. Bohlen, *Transformation of American Foreign Policy*, p. 86.
58. In the memorandum cited in n. 25, Russell reports to Benton on the interest Acheson and other high policy officers displayed in the reports of the Public Studies Division.
59. See n. 25 above.
60. William R. Caspary, "United States Public Opinion during the Onset of the Cold War," *Peace Research Society Papers* 9 (1968); William A. Gamson and André Modigliani, *Untangling the Cold War: A Strategy for Testing Rival Theories* (Boston, 1971).
61. Department of State, Monthly Survey of American Opinion on International Affairs, March 1947.
62. May, *Lessons" of the Past*.
63. George Kennan, *Memoirs, 1925-1950* (New York, 1969), p. 332.
64. Jones, *Fifteen Weeks*, p. 150.
65. Kolko and Kolko, *Limits of Power*, p. 334.
66. See n. 25 above.
67. Ibid.
68. See Lentner, "Concept of Crisis."
69. May writes, "Truman and his advisers always doubted whether their decisions would command public support." May, *"Lessons" of the Past*, p. 48.

6
Afterword

Senator Vandenberg thought that there was a parallel in the clash between nazism and democracy in the 1930s and between communism and democracy in the 1940s. [1] The parallel consisted in an image of aggressive totalitarianism and the folly of appeasement. This image was widely held by those who were attentive to foreign policy in 1947 and helps to explain the rapidity with which President Truman convinced the Congress and the American people of the need to expend treasure and, before long, blood in the defense of free institutions. Few questioned the wholesale transfer of the image of totalitarianism from Nazi to Soviet society. [2] The press regularly referred to the Truman Doctrine as the antitotalitarian aid program, a phrase that required no quotation marks.

Serious questioning of the analogy was extremely unorthodox and particularly unpalatable when voiced by those, such as former Vice-President Henry Wallace, who were regarded by those on the right as sympathetic to bolshevism. Wallace's criticisms of the Truman Doctrine, all the more abrasive when uttered in Britain—whose abdication had been the proximate cause of the doctrine's formulation—were explicitly compared with Colonel Charles Lindbergh's alleged sabotage of Roosevelt's quarantine proposal ten years earlier. A young congressman from Texas, Lyndon B. Johnson, upheld both the quarantine speech and the Truman Doctrine speech against "isolationists" new and old:

A former Vice-President is crying out against the course charted by President Truman in his message to Congress in louder language than Colonel Lindbergh protested the policy proclaimed by President Roosevelt in his historic Chicago speech. Can it be that this former Vice-President believes that it is right to quarantine the aggressors if they are Fascists, but wrong if they are Communists; and does Colonel Lindbergh reason conversely? As for myself I care not whether an aggressor be Communist or Fascist.[3]

Most of Johnson's colleagues agreed with him, as witnessed by their successive endorsement of aid to Greece and Turkey, the Marshall Plan, NATO, and other milestones of American foreign policy in the cold war.

The accretion of presidential power during the war, coupled with the ubiquitous acceptance of the appeasement analogy after it, drew a new line between the executive and the legislature in foreign affairs. Whereas Roosevelt declined to challenge legislative preeminence in 1937, Truman faced a quiescent Congress a decade later. The Republican Congress of 1947 was capable of astonishing acts of self-abnegation in the name of a bipartisan drive to prevent another Munich. Senator Vandenberg won applause from his colleagues when he urged the following in support of rapid endorsement of executive decision: "Congress does not enjoy original jurisdiction in foreign relations. That is the prerogative of the Chief Executive."[4] Such a self-denying ordinance, blasphemy a decade earlier, is stunning testimony to the resurgence of executive power in foreign policy.

The force of the appeasement analogy and the rise of an "imperial presidency" undoubtedly furnish a partial explanation of Truman's rapid success in mobilizing support for his doctrine in 1947. But it has been the thesis of this book that neither development provides a sufficient explanation of the change in presidential prerogatives since the 1930s. The missing factor, as every reader who has persevered this far will have divined, is the transformation of the opinion-policy relationship. The president's sense of the possible had grown with his capacity to invoke his own separate constituency, the mass public. This capacity depended on the existence of linkages that liberated the White House from dependence on congressional or other surrogates for popular opinion. In 1937 virtually no mechanism existed for the scientific analysis of opinion data and its regular transmission to the White House. Nor were there branches of the foreign-policy bureaucracy specifically charged with the mobilization of support for government initiatives. The war changed this situation drastically. A succession of emergency agencies acted as intermediaries between the executive and the public. Hadley Cantril, the seminal figure in convincing policy makers of the relevance of poll data to their work, opened up additional informal channels. The State Department was heir to much of the experience and many of the personnel involved in opinion-information work during the war. The specter of isolationism and Wilson's failure with the League combined to inject public affairs into the heart of postwar planning.

This analysis seems to support the argument that, far from being constrained by popular opinion, policy makers manipulate it in support of their predetermined policy choices. Truman defined the situation in March 1947 in terms calculated to arouse popular support. He made use of opinion experts to an unprecedented degree in formulating and promoting the Truman Doctrine. This campaign instilled a new sense of America's responsibility for maintaining world order.

But this "classic case" of manipulation reveals a circularity of reasoning that is fatal to the radical argument, for the need to mobilize consent is itself witness to the constraint that national leaders perceive as inhering in the mass public. It would make no sense to spend vast resources on persuading the public unless popular support is seen as a necessary condition of a policy's success. The Truman Doctrine was adapted in its early stages to elicit a favorable public response. The ideological tone and global framework of the doctrine, while matching the convictions of Truman's advisers, were designed to capture the public's imagination.[5] It was deemed necessary to modify the reliance on collective security that the State Department had done so much to promote in 1944 and 1945.

This touches on another flaw in the manipulation argument. Fine tuning of mass opinion is a patent impossibility. The instruments for mobilizing consent, though comparatively sophisticated in the postwar period, remain crude and imperfect. It is impossible to achieve just enough public enthusiasm to sustain the current initiative without setting up false expectations for the future. "In democratic societies . . . one of the most outstanding features is that national leadership is confronted with the public opinion it had helped to crystallize at earlier points in time."[6] The premonitions of those who had urged a soft sell of collective security in 1944 were realized in the need for a hard sell of selective security in 1947. The government's very success in permeating shared images with the doctrine of containment returned to delay rapprochement with erstwhile adversaries, notably China. Yesterday's manipulation is today's constraint. An adroit piece of persuasion today will return to limit options the day after tomorrow.

This tendency is exacerbated in a country historically unsuited to accepting national interest as the basis for its foreign policy. The hopes raised by doctrines cast in more inspirational terms come back to haunt national leaders when the realities of international politics catch up with them. Each time this happens a new national debate is called for to dispel lessons that have been learned only too well.

The consensus established in the late 1940s was not seriously challenged until the late 1960s or early 1970s. During the 1950s politics as usual prevailed within the cold war framework. Foreign-policy choices were tactical rather than strategic. This does not gainsay Joseph McCarthy or John Foster Dulles. But "roll back" versus "containment" was a tactical, not to say spurious, rather than a strategic choice. In the absence of a challenge to shared images, intolerable costs to the average American, or the intrusion of foreign policy into daily life,[7] opportunities for public involvement in decision making declined. The slackening of the linkages between the executive and the public was symbolized by Congress's success in liquidating the State Department's polling operations in 1957.[8]

American war casualties and tax surcharges brought foreign policy back into daily life in the 1960s. America's costly failure in Vietnam shattered shared images of the country's place in the world. Withdrawal from Indochina, détente with the Soviet Union, and rapprochement with China occurred only after a new, and less altruistic, doctrine had been formulated, packaged, and sold to the American people. The Nixon doctrine, for all its cool and rational analysis of America's relations with its allies, was designed primarily to mobilize domestic support for a new reorientation in American foreign policy.

The conclusions of this study validate neither the radical nor the traditional model of the opinion policy relationship. The traditional scholar is naive in the belief that democratic policy makers eschew manipulation. But the radical scholar is equally naive, or disingenuous, in arguing that manipulation necessarily succeeds. On the contrary, shared images, especially those promoted by government at an earlier time, return to constrain later options. Policies are often modified at an early and inconspicuous stage in their formulation to overcome this constraint. The participation of the outer circles of opinion in policy making does not fall neatly into the category of manipulation or constraint. The form of participation, as well as its probability, is determined by a complex set of factors, some of which have been identified in this analysis.

NOTES

1. Vandenberg to R. F. Moffett of Flint, Michigan, May 12, 1947, in Arthur H. Vandenberg Jr., *The Private Papers of Senator Vandenberg* (Boston, 1952), pp. 341-342.
2. This transfer has come under fire in recent years from scholars who have attempted to adopt a behavioral approach to the study of the Soviet Union and so to arrive at some other characterization of its social and political system. Fredrick Fleron, *Communist Studies and the Social Sciences* (New York, 1969); H. G. Skilling and F. Griffiths, *Interest Groups in Soviet Politics* (Princeton, 1971). This rejection of the concept of totalitarianism was part of the liberal intellectual reaction to the apparently misleading application of the appeasement analogy to Southeast Asia. Perhaps a resuscitation of the concept might be predicted as authoritarian communist regimes come to power in Indochina during the 1970s.
3. *Congressional Record*, 80th Cong., 1st sess., p. 4696.
4. Ibid., p. 3198.
5. Truman was not yet a self-confident president, and, before the March 12 speech, few doubted that he was a lame duck. He therefore had an additional incentive to have a bold and inspiring foreign policy initiative associated with his presidency.
6. Amitai Etzioni, "The Kennedy Experiment," *Western Political Quarterly* (June 1967): 361-380.
7. The exception was, of course, the Korean War; but as a response to overt aggression the war fit comfortably into the concept of containment. It did not therefore precipitate the kind of national debate that accompanied the Indochina involvement.
8. The House Committee on Government Operations ordered an investigation of the State Department's polling operation after a leak of poll figures to the press. The department was accused of illegally using the polls for purposes of publicity or propaganda. It abandoned its contracts with polling organizations because of the furor even before formal hearings were held. Robert Ellsworth Elder, *The Policy Machine: The Department of State and American Foreign Policy* (Syracuse, 1960), pp. 145-146.

Bibliography

ARCHIVES AND MANUSCRIPT COLLECTIONS

CANTRIL, HADLEY. The Roper Public Opinion Research Center, Williams College, Williamstown, Massachusetts.

DAVIS, ELMER. The Library of Congress, Washington, D.C.

HOPKINS, HARRY L. Franklin D. Roosevelt Library, Hyde Park, New York.

HULL, CORDELL. The Library of Congress, Washington, D.C.

JONES, JOSEPH M. Harry S. Truman Library, Independence, Missouri.

MACLEISH, ARCHIBALD. The Library of Congress, Washington, D.C.

Motion Picture Division. The Library of Congress, Washington, D.C.

Office of Public Affairs Files. Department of State, Washington, D.C.

Office of War Information Archives. Federal Record Center, National Archives, Suitland, Maryland.

PASVOLSKY, LEO. The Library of Congress, Washington, D.C.

Public Opinion Poll Archives. The Roper Center for Public Opinion Research, Williams College, Williamstown, Massachusetts.

ROOSEVELT, FRANKLIN D. Franklin D. Roosevelt Library, Hyde Park, New York.

STETTINIUS, EDWARD R., JR. University of Virginia Library, Charlottesville, Virginia.

OFFICIAL DOCUMENTS

U.S. Congress. *Congressional Record.*

U.S. House of Representatives. Subcommittee of the Committee on Appropriations.
———. Subcommittee of the Committee on Appropriations. *Hearings on HR 296811.* 78th Cong., 1st sess., 1943.
U.S. Department of State, *Peace and War: United States Foreign Policy, 1931-1941.* Washington D.C., 1943.
Hearings on the National War Agencies Appropriation Bill for 1944. 78th Cong. 1st sess., 1943.
U.S. Senate. Committee on Foreign Relations. *Nominations—Department of State.* 78th Cong., 2d sess., 1944.
———. Committee on Foreign Relations. *Hearings on a Bill to Provide for Assistance to Greece and Turkey.* 80th Cong., 1st sess., 1947.
U.S. Government. *Code of Federal Regulations, 1938-1943.* Title 3, 1968.

INTERVIEWS

John Sloan Dickey. Hanover, New Hampshire. April 17, 1973.
Francis Russell. Medford, Massachusetts. May 7, 1973.

NEWSPAPERS AND MAGAZINES

Atlanta Constitution.
Atlantic Monthly.
Boston Herald.
Chicago Tribune.
Cincinnati Enquirer.
Des Moines Register.
Fortune.
Louisville Courier-Journal (Kentucky).
New York Herald Tribune.
New York Times.
Philadelphia Inquirer.
Pioneer Press (St. Paul).
Washington Post.
Washington Star News.

BOOKS

ACHESON, DEAN. *Present at the Creation: My Years in the State Department.* New York, 1969.
ALMOND, GABRIEL. *The American People and Foreign Policy.* New York, 1950
AMBROSE, STEPHEN E. *Rise to Globalism: American Foreign Policy, 1934-1970.* Baltimore, 1971.

BAILEY, THOMAS A. *The Man in the Street: The Impact of American Public Opinion on Foreign Policy.* New York, 1948.

BARNET, RICHARD J. *Roots of War: The Men and Institutions behind U.S. Foreign Policy.* Baltimore, 1971.

BARRON, GLORIA. *Leadership in Crisis.* New York, 1973.

BEARD, CHARLES A. *American Foreign Policy in the Making, 1932-1940.* New Haven, 1946.

BEST, JAMES J. *Public Opinion Micro and Macro.* Homewood, Illinois, 1973.

BLUM, JOHN M. *From the Morgenthau Diaries.* Boston, 1959.

BOGART, LEO. *Silent Politics: Polls and the Awareness of Public Opinion.* New York, 1972.

BOHLEN, CHARLES E. *The Transformation of American Foreign Policy.* New York, 1969.

BRUNER, JEROME S. *Mandate from the People.* New York, 1944.

BRYCE, JAMES. *Modern Democracies.* New York, 1921.

BURLINGAME, ROGER. *Don't Let Them Scare You: The Life and Times of Elmer Davis.* Philadelphia, 1961.

BURNS, JAMES MACGREGOR. *Roosevelt: The Lion and the Fox.* New York, 1956.

———. *Roosevelt: The Soldier of Freedom.* New York, 1970.

CAMPBELL, THOMAS M. *Masquerade Peace: America's U.N. Policy, 1944-1945.* Tallahassee, Florida, 1973.

CANTRIL, HADLEY. *Gauging Public Opinion.* Princeton, *1944.*

———, and STRUNK, MILDRED. *Public Opinion, 1935-1946.* Princeton, 1951.

CLAUDE, INIS L. *Swords into Plowshares: The Problems and Progress of International Organization.* New York, 1964.

CLEMENS, DIANE SHAVER. *Yalta.* New York, 1970.

COHEN, BERNARD C. *The Press and Foreign Policy.* Princeton, 1963.

———. *The Public's Impact on Foreign Policy.* Boston, 1973.

CORNWELL, ELMER E., JR. *Presidential Leadership of Public Opinion.* Bloomington, 1965.

CREEL, GEORGE. *Complete Report of the Chairman of the Committee on Public Information.* Washington D.C., 1920.

———. *How We Advertised America.* New York, 1920.

DIVINE, ROBERT A. *The Illusion of Neutrality.* Chicago, 1962.

———. *Roosevelt and World War II.* Baltimore, 1969.

———. *Second Chance: The Triumph of Internationalism in America During World War II.* New York, 1967.

EDWARDS, JEROME E. *The Foreign Policy of Col. McCormick's Tribune.* Reno, 1971.

FARRELL, JOHN C., and SMITH, ASA P., eds. *Image and Reality in World Politics.* New York, 1967.

FERRELL, ROBERT H. *The American Secretaries of State and Their Diplomacy.* New York, 1965.

FILENE, PETER G. *Americans and the Soviet Experiment, 1917-1933: American Attitude towards Russia from the February Revolution until Diplomatic Recognition.* Cambridge, Massachusetts, 1967.

FLERON, FREDRICK. *Communist Studies and the Social Sciences.* New York, 1969.

FONTAINE, ANDRÉ. *History of the Cold War.* New York, 1968.

GADDIS, JOHN LEWIS. *The United States and the Origins of the Cold War, 1941-1947.* New York, 1972.

GAMSON, WILLIAM A., and MODIGLIANI, ANDRÉ. *Untangling the Cold War: A Strategy for Testing Rival Theories.* Boston, 1971.

GARDNER, LLOYD C. *Architects of Illusion: Men and Ideas in American Foreign Policy, 1941-1949.* Chicago, 1970.

GEORGE, ALEXANDER, and GEORGE, JULIET. *Woodrow Wilson and Colonel House: A Personality Study.* New York, 1956.

GRAEBNER, NORMAN A. *An Uncertain Tradition: American Secretaries of State in the Twentieth Century.* New York, 1961.

HALPERIN, MORTON H. *Bureaucratic Politics and Foreign Policy.* Washington, D.C., 1974.

———, and KANTER, ARNOLD. *Readings in American Foreign Policy: A Bureaucratic Perspective.* Boston, 1973.

HERMANN, CHARLES F. *International Crisis: Insights from Behavioral Research.* New York, 1972.

HILSMAN, ROGER. *To Move a Nation.* Garden City, 1967.

HOROWITZ, DAVID. *The Free World Colossus: A Critique of American Foreign Policy in the Cold War,* rev. ed. New York, 1971.

HULL, CORDELL. *The Memoirs of Cordell Hull.* New York, 1948.

HUNTINGTON, SAMUEL P. *The Common Defense: Strategic Programs in National Politics.* New York, 1961.

HYMAN, HERBERT H. *Secondary Analysis of Sample Surveys.* New York, 1972.

ICKES, HAROLD L. *The Secret Diary of Harold L. Ickes.* New York, 1954.

JONAS, MANFRED. *Isolationism in America, 1935-1941.* Ithaca, 1966.

JONES, JOSEPH M. *The Fifteen Weeks.* New York, 1955.

JOHNSON, WALTER. *The Battle Against Isolation.* Chicago, 1944.

KATZ, ELIHU, and LAZARSFELD, PAUL. *Personal Influence: The Part Played by People in the Flow of Mass Communications.* New York, 1955.

KENNAN, GEORGE F. *Memoirs, 1925-1950.* Boston, 1967.

KOLKO, GABRIEL. *The Politics of War: The World and United States Foreign Policy, 1943-1945.* New York, 1968.

———, and KOLKO, JOYCE. *The Limits of Power: The World and United States Foreign Policy, 1945-1954.* New York, 1972.

LANDECKER, MANFRED. *The President and Public Opinion; Leadership in Foreign Affairs.* Washington D.C., 1968.

LARSON, CEDRIC, and MOCK, JAMES R. *Words That Won the War: The Story of the Committee on Public Information, 1917-1919.* Princeton, 1939.

LASSWELL, HAROLD. *Propaganda Technique in World War I.* Cambridge, Massachusetts, 1971. Originally published as *Propaganda Technique in the World War.* London, 1927.

LIPPMANN, WALTER. *The Public Philosophy.* Boston, 1955.

MADDOX, ROBERT JAMES. *The New Left and the Origins of the Cold War.* Princeton, 1973.

MARKEL, LESTER, ed. *Public Opinion and Foreign Policy.* New York, 1949.

MAY, ERNEST R. *"Lessons" of the Past: The Use and Misuse of History in American Foreign Policy.* New York, 1973.

MILLIS, WALTER, ed. *The Forrestal Diaries*. New York, 1951.

MUELLER, JOHN E. *War, Presidents and Public Opinion*. New York, 1973.

NEUSTADT, RICHARD. *Alliance Politics*. New York, 1970.

———. *Presidential Power: The Politics of Leadership*. New York, 1960.

NOTTER, HARLEY F. *Postwar Foreign Policy Planning*, Washington D.C., 1949.

PRICE, DON K., ed. *The Secretary of State*. Englewood Cliffs, 1960.

RIVERA, JOSEPH DE. *The Psychological Dimension of Foreign Policy*. Columbus, Ohio, 1968.

ROLL, CHARLES W., JR., and CANTRIL, ALBERT H. *Polls: Their Use and Misuse in Politics*. New York, 1972.

ROOSEVELT, ELLIOT. *FDR, His Personal Letters, 1928-1945*. New York, 1950.

ROPER, ELMO. *You and Your Leaders: Their Actions and Your Reactions*. New York, 1957.

ROSENAU, J. N. *International Politics and Foreign Policy*. New York, 1969.

———. *National Leadership and Foreign Policy*. Princeton, 1963.

———. *Public Opinion and Foreign Policy*. New York, 1961.

———, ed. *Domestic Sources of Foreign Policy*. New York, 1967.

SCHELLING, THOMAS C. *The Strategy of Conflict*. Oxford, 1970.

SCHILLING, WARNER R.; HAMMOND, PAUL Y.; and SNYDER, GLENN H. *Strategy, Politics and Defense Budgets*. New York, 1962.

SCHLESINGER, ARTHUR M., JR. *The Bitter Heritage: Vietnam and American Democracy*. Boston, 1966.

———. *The Imperial Presidency*. New York, 1974.

SKILLING, H. GORDON, and GRIFFITHS, F. *Interest Groups in Soviet Politics*. Princeton, 1971.

SMALL, MELVIN, ed. *Public Opinions and Historians*. Detroit, 1970.

SNYDER, RICHARD C., and FURNISS, EDGAR S., JR. *American Foreign Policy*. New York, 1954.

SORENSON, THEODORE C. *Decision-Making in the White House*. New York, 1963.

SPROUT, HAROLD, and SPROUT, MARGARET. *Toward a Politics of the Planet Earth*. New York, 1971.

STOESSINGER, JOHN. *Nations in Darkness*. New York, 1971.

STUART, GRAHAM H. *The Department of State*. New York, 1949.

Survey Research Center, University of Michigan. *Public Attitudes Towards American Foreign Policy*. Ann Arbor, 1947.

ULAM, ADAM B. *Expansion and Coexistence*. New York, 1968.

VANDENBERG, ARTHUR H., JR. *The Private Papers of Senator Vandenberg*. Boston, 1952.

WILLIAMS, WILLIAM A. *The Tragedy of American Diplomacy*. New York, 1962.

ARTICLES

ALLISON, GRAHAM T., and HALPERIN, MORTON H. "Bureaucratic Politics: A Paradigm and Some Policy Implications." In Tanter, Raymond, and Ullman, Richard H., eds., *Theory and Policy in International Relations*. Princeton, 1972.

BERELSON, BERNARD. "Democratic Theory and Public Opinion." *Public Opinion Quarterly* (Fall 1952).

BORG, DOROTHY. "Notes on Roosevelt's 'Quarantine' Speech." *Political Science Quarterly* 3 (1957).

CASPARY, WILLIAM R. "The Mood Theory." *American Political Science Review* (June 1970).

———. "United States Public Opinion During the Onset of the Cold War." *Peace Research Society Papers* 9 (1968).

COHEN, BERNARD C. "The Relationship between Public Opinion and the Foreign Policy Maker." In Melvin Small, ed., *Public Opinion and Historians.* Detroit, 1970.

COLEGROVE, KENNETH. "The Role of Congress and Public Opinion in Formulating Foreign Policy." *American Political Science* (October 1944).

DICKEY, JOHN SLOAN. "The Secretary and the American Public." In Price, Don K., ed., *The Secretary of State.* Englewood Cliffs, 1960.

FELLER, A. H. "OWI on the Home Front." *Public Opinion Quarterly* (Spring 1943).

FOSTER, H. SCHUYLER. "American Public Opinion and U.S. Foreign Policy." *Department of State Bulletin* (November 30, 1959).

FREE, LLOYD A. "The Introversion-Extroversion Cycle in National Mood in Recent Decades." Prepared for delivery at the annual conference of the American Association for Public Opinion Research, May 1973.

HARDING, T. SWANN. "Genesis of One 'Government Propaganda Mill.'" *Public Opinion Quarterly* (Summer 1947).

———. "Information Techniques of the Department of Agriculture." *Public Opinion Quarterly* (Winter 1936).

HERMANN, CHARLES F. "Some Issues in the Study of International Crisis." in Hermann, Charles, ed., *International Crisis: Insights from Behavioral Research.* New York, 1972.

HOLSTI, OLE. "Cognitive Dynamics and Images of the Enemy." In Farrell, John C., and Smith, Asa P., *Image and Reality in World Politics.* New York, 1967.

KANE, R. KEITH. "The OFF." *Public Opinion Quarterly* (Summer 1942).

KRIESBERG, MARTIN. "Dark Areas of Ignorance." In Markel, Lester, ed., *Public Opinion and Foreign Policy.* New York, 1949.

———. "What Congressmen and Administrators Think of the Polls." *Public Opinion Quarterly* (Fall 1945).

LARSON, CEDRIC. "The British Ministry of Information." *Public Opinion Quarterly* (Fall 1941).

LAVES, WALTER, H.C., and WILCOX, FRANCIS O. "The State Department Continues its Reorganization." *American Political Science Review* (April 1945).

LEIGH, MICHAEL. "Review: Bernard C. Cohen, The Public's Impact on Foreign Policy." *Political Science Quarterly* (September 1974).

LENTNER, HOWARD H. "The Concept of Crisis as Viewed by the United States Department of State." In Hermann, Charles F., *International Crisis: Insights from Behavioral Research.* New York, 1972.

LEWIS, ANTHONY DEXTER. "What Do Congressmen Hear: The Mail." *Public Opinion Quarterly* (Spring 1956).

MARKEL, LESTER. "Opinion a Neglected Instrument," In Markel, Lester, ed., *Public Opinion and Foreign Policy,* New York, 1949.

MELLETT, LOWELL. "Government Propaganda." *Atlantic Monthly* (September 1941).

MORSE, EDWARD L. "The Transformation of Foreign Policies." *World Politics* (April 1970).

RIGGS, ROBERT E. "Overselling the U.N. Charter: Fact and Myth." *International Organization* (Spring 1960).

SINGER, J. DAVID. "The Level-of-Analysis Problem in International Relations." In Rosenau, J. N., ed., *International Politics and Foreign Policy.* New York, 1969.

WATT, DONALD. "Roosevelt and Chamberlain: Two Appeasers." *International Journal* (Spring 1973).

WILLIAMS, MARGARET HICKS. "'The President's' Office of Government Reports," *Public Opinion Quarterly* (Winter 1941).

Index

ABOUT THE AUTHOR

Michael Leigh, Tutor in International Relations at the University of Sussex in England, was educated at Oxford University and the Massachusetts Institute of Technology. His research and writing focus on the politics of detente and Common Market issues.